THE SULTA

Mark Killick is a senior producer
programme. He has also worked fo
Action and Thames Television's *City* television
credits include *Project Babylon – Sada* *gun*, showing British
involvement in the giant gun, *The Max Factor*, an exposé of Robert
Maxwell's share support operation and *Lady Porter – The Pursuit of
Power*, which revealed corruption in Westminster Council. During
the past three years Mark Killick has won a number of national
television awards including the Royal Television Society's award for
the best home current affairs programme and the Broadcasting Press
Guild's award for best single documentary. He also writes for both
newspapers and magazines and specializes in financial investigations.
The Sultan of Sleaze is his first book and it follows up his controversial
World in Action programme on David Sullivan.

THE SULTAN OF SLEAZE

THE INSIDE STORY OF DAVID SULLIVAN'S
SEX AND MEDIA EMPIRE

MARK KILLICK

PENGUIN BOOKS

PENGUIN BOOKS

Published by the Penguin Group
Penguin Books Ltd, 27 Wrights Lane, London w8 5tz, England
Penguin Books USA Inc., 375 Hudson Street, New York, New York 10014, USA
Penguin Books Australia Ltd, Ringwood, Victoria, Australia
Penguin Books Canada Ltd, 10 Alcorn Avenue, Toronto, Ontario, Canada m4v 3b2
Penguin Books (NZ) Ltd, 182–190 Wairau Road, Auckland 10, New Zealand

Penguin Books Ltd, Registered Offices: Harmondsworth, Middlesex, England

First published 1994
1 3 5 7 9 10 8 6 4 2

Filmset in 10/12pt Monophoto Garamond
Printed in England by Clays Ltd, St Ives plc

'I've never had a problem, only opportunities.'

David Sullivan

CONTENTS

ACKNOWLEDGEMENTS

This book is a continuation of an investigation begun in the spring of 1992 by Granada Television's *World in Action* team. The resulting programme, which I produced and directed, was transmitted on 21 September 1992 and watched by almost ten million people, representing 45 per cent of the available audience. This substantial figure suggests that many people want to know more about David Sullivan; what you are now about to read is the first serious attempt to chronicle his life.

There are many people who have contributed to this project with their talents, time and knowledge and I would like to thank them all. If anyone, through oversight, is not mentioned then please accept my humble apologies.

The Granada Television team that initially backed the programme is at the top of the list of people who deserve my thanks. There were three programme editors involved and all of them contributed to the investigation. The programme was commissioned by Nick Hayes, who always believed in it and supported it unfalteringly, even when progress was slow. It was taken to air by Dianne Nelmes, who gave it the plum slot at the start of a new series. Finally, its transfer to book form was generously agreed by Charles Tremayne. I would also like to thank Ray Fitzwalter, who as head of Granada's news and current affairs department oversaw the whole production, and Claire Powell, the programme researcher, who did an excellent job throughout. It is a matter of regret to me that she was unable to co-author this book.

After the programme was transmitted, I returned to the BBC's *Panorama* programme and I am grateful to the team there, too, for their help and support. In particular, I would like to mention *Panorama*'s editor, Glenwyn Benson, who allowed me the time to complete this project. I would also like to thank the contributors who went out of their way to ensure I got the story right. Paul Price spent several days explaining to me how the Private Shops were restructured and John East spent as much time again taking me through David Sullivan's film career. In addition to all the above, I would like to express my gratitude to the many journalists whose stories now lie gathering dust in the cuttings libraries of the Press Association and the BBC; without these stories it would have been almost impossible to complete this task.

Finally, I would like to thank all those who have helped me in the actual process of writing this, my first book. Thanks must go to my agent, Carol Heaton, for having the faith to invest her time and effort in me in the first place, and to Tony Lacey at Penguin who put up with far more than he deserved. Thanks are also due to Wendy Darabi-Fard and Maria Ellis for transcribing my many long and rambling interviews and last, but by no means least, to CK and DK for simply being there.

INTRODUCTION

When this investigation began, in early 1992, David Sullivan was still aggressively expanding his operations. Besides owning the *Daily Sport* and *Sunday Sport*, 10 per cent of the Bristol Evening Post and 3 per cent of Transworld Communications, he was also preparing to launch another newspaper, the *News and Echo*.

Since then his advance has slowed. The circulation of all his papers has fallen, he has sold his stake in the Bristol Evening Post, and new restrictions on adult telephone lines further threaten his finances. Against this, he has acquired a £5 million cash pile, launched his new paper and bought Birmingham City Football Club. In addition, records show that in the year ending 30 September 1992 Sullivan spent £3.7 million increasing his property portfolio yet still managed to pay himself a salary of over £1 million.

David Sullivan is now living in his new £6 million palace, plotting his next move and waiting to see if the charm offensive he launched in 1992 will pay off. He wants to be a media mogul and he wants to be respectable and he knows the two are inextricably linked. His new paper and even his magnificent new home are all part of this long-term strategy. Sullivan is currently biding his time but it won't be long before he starts to advance again.

David Sullivan has wanted nothing to do with this book and he has refused to see me or discuss its contents. His closest associates have also refused to be interviewed. Nevertheless, I have done all I can to ensure what is said is not only accurate but fair. Should anybody reading this book be in a position to provide more information on any of the people or events mentioned, I would be delighted to hear from them.

Mark Killick,
December 1993

CHAPTER ONE

THE MAN WHO COLLECTS WOMEN

Birch Hall is Britain's newest stately home. It stands in its own grounds just outside the little village of Theydon Bois in Essex and in its neo-Georgian splendour it has often been compared to Buckingham Palace. It was commissioned by David Sullivan, one of the country's most successful and controversial businessmen. It cost a staggering £6 million to build, making it one of the most expensive private houses to be completed this century. Even the carpets are said to be worth £195 per square yard.

For David Sullivan, the opulence of Birch Hall is a calculated gesture of defiance aimed at all those who have tried to stop him over the years. It serves as an impressive reminder to everyone that he has won through despite the opposition of the police, the press and nearly the whole of the British establishment. His achievements are now, literally, set in marble and stone.

Just twenty of David Sullivan's closest friends were invited to the housewarming party at Birch Hall. Because of the symbolic importance he attached to the occasion, limousines were sent to collect them all. Everyone was asked to arrive by six-thirty, as Sullivan abandoned late nights long ago in favour of an altogether more sedate lifestyle.

The atmosphere of sophisticated refinement was set as soon as the guests drew up outside Birch Hall's magnificent columned entrance. Everyone was smartly dressed and Sullivan himself greeted them at the door and ushered them into the huge entrance hall. The gentle strains of 'These Foolish Things' could be heard in the background, played by a string quartet located in the minstrels' gallery. Once everyone had assembled and drinks had been served, David Sullivan and Karren Brady, then his girlfriend, began conducting the grandest of grand tours.

No one who goes round Birch Hall can fail to be impressed. In the basement is a computerized ten-pin-bowling alley, a Stringfellow's-style dance-floor complete with glitter ball and a bar equipped with television, video and SIS (for screening live horse-racing). Just around the corner is an indoor swimming pool, a solarium and a jacuzzi, with French windows opening on to an Oriental garden and, beyond that, a deer park.

Marble flooring gives the reception areas a feeling of belonging to an earlier, more glorious, era and even the cornices are decorated with griffins and urns. They echo the design of Sullivan's crest, *Per Laborum Ad Honorum*, which decorates the spectacular entrance and means 'through hard work to honour'. The long dining hall seats twenty-six comfortably and there is a full-size snooker room for those who play. The whole house is spotless throughout. Sullivan is obsessive about cleanliness and doesn't smoke or drink, though he is hopelessly addicted to chocolate. Since his father died of lung cancer a few years ago, his mother, Thelma, spends an increasing amount of her time staying at Birch Hall.

This palatial new mansion has no less than three kitchens and ten upstairs bedrooms, each one named after a racecourse. David Sullivan's huge master suite is called Sandown, because that is his favourite course. Two en-suite bathrooms are attached to it, one with a scallop-shaped bath designed for up to four people just in case 'I get lucky or married'.[1] Sullivan has summed up his feelings for his new palace with a masterly display of understatement. 'It's a pretty house ... I wanted it modern and fairly bright in an oldy way. And it's nicely finished. I'm really quite proud of it.'[2]

Despite the relatively small number of guests at the housewarming, place settings were used to add to the general air of refinement. As Sullivan looked at the cards and decided the final seating positions, three names in particular must have set him thinking about the past. Only he and they could really know his whole incredible rags-to-riches story.

Christine King is probably the most knowledgeable of all. She now administers his old Private Shop sex empire through a company called Limetime Services. King first worked for David Sullivan as a secretary in 1975 and has remained fiercely loyal to him ever since. She once said of Conegate, a key Sullivan company, 'It is like a baby to me. I was in at the birth.'[3]

David Sullivan's older brother, Clive, is another who can legitimately claim to know the truth. He is Conegate's managing director and the second shareholder in Limetime Services. It is rumoured that it was the relative grandeur of his own home that finally provoked his brother into building the magnificent Birch Hall.

The third person who could probably tell the whole story is Brian Richards, a former Ford worker and the man who supposedly purchased the Private Shops from Sullivan in 1982. These three, along with his best friend, Harry Gorman, and his business partners, David and Ralph Gold, make up David Sullivan's inner circle. Between them they control much of Britain's sex industry.

The guests were entertained during dinner by a fifteen-piece orchestra and a cabaret singer performing old Cole Porter and George Gershwin numbers. The mood was one of satisfaction all round. Despite considerable adversity, David Sullivan had finally become part of Britain's élite, if not part of the establishment.

As the dishes were cleared and coffee was served, Sullivan decided that the occasion could not pass without at least a few words being said. Not a born speaker, he kept things short and to the point. This was, he declared, the most important night of his life and he was pleased to have shared it with his closest friends.

John East, a long-time confidant of Sullivan and a BBC radio broadcaster, had, like most of the guests, been touched by the whole evening and particularly by those few words that so obviously came from the heart. A reply was clearly needed and, by common consent, it seemed right that he should give it. He stood up, gathered his thoughts for a moment and began.

'I've known David for close on twenty years. I remember our first meeting in his small office over a shop in Upton Lane. On that occasion he was brisk and to the point. A tough guy, I thought, modelled no doubt on James Cagney or Edward G. Robinson. But, as I gained his confidence, the façade evaporated and there emerged a whimsical man who was generous and kindly disposed to all those who treated him fairly. The humanity with David Sullivan extended to crossing London during a busy day to reassure my dying mother that, if her son was ever in need, he would lend a helping hand. All admirable characteristics for a man who has been the butt of media criticism for as long as he has been in the big time. I once felt the need to write to David and said, "Your success proves that he travels the fastest who travels alone." Birch Hall is a monument at the end of the jungle. I've only been on the sidelines of your life. All I can do is wish you well and thank you for everything.'

It was a generous and genuinely moving speech that was well received by all the guests. But not everyone sees David Sullivan in such a kind and affectionate way. When he first moved to Theydon Bois, many of the villagers were more than a little concerned about his reputation. They were worried that living next door to Britain's most notorious porn king might prove over-stimulating. Sullivan, though, anxious to be a good neighbour, did his best to explain how things had changed.

'I think they were a bit nervous,' he told an inquisitive reporter. 'They imagined I was going to have wild parties. My parties are quiet and the house is so isolated people don't know they're going on. The last thing I want to do is offend people. I live a very conservative lifestyle. I'm very ordinary and don't have wild orgies. I don't drink and don't take drugs, though my friends drink. That's why I only have a maximum of twenty-four people; if people get drunk you can control that number, but, if you have 100 people and they get drunk, I'd have my house wrecked.'[4]

The *Sunday Times* now claims that David Sullivan is one of the richest men in Britain. His private company accounts show that, in the year ending September 1991, his best year, he managed to pay himself a salary of almost £2 million and he is now thought to be worth about £150 million. He owns 50 per cent of Sport Newspapers, the company that publishes the *Daily Sport* and *Sunday Sport* and recently launched the northern *News and Echo*. He also has a stake in the radio group Transworld Communications and admits still to running several soft-porn magazines and some premium-rate adult telephone lines, and to distributing the occasional sex film from his back catalogue.

Peter Grimsditch, a former editor of the *Daily Sport* and a well-respected figure in Fleet Street, believes that David Sullivan could become Britain's next media mogul. He told *World in Action*, the Granada Television programme that spent four months investigating Sullivan, 'I think he could be a very big tycoon. It will be necessary for the nearly all-powerful establishment to accept him as an extremely astute businessman, that could put a limitation on him, but watch out Murdoch, wait till he starts buying papers in America.'[5]

Grimsditch, who still worked for the *Daily Sport* at the time, went on to outline Sullivan's ambitious plans for the future. 'Our aim,' he said, 'is to have two national dailies and two national Sundays. I don't think we'll ever have as many employees as Express Newspapers but hopefully we'll sell more newspapers.'[6]

It's a prospect that genuinely alarms some other newspapermen who have seen David Sullivan's operations at first hand. David Buchan was sacked from the *Daily Star* during its link-up with the *Sunday Sport* for saying it had become 'a soft-porn rag'. Buchan believes that David Sullivan will always go for the lowest common denominator in his ruthless pursuit of profit. 'He's not a philanthropist. He's out to make money. He's made money out of *Sunday Sport*, he's made money out of Miss Whiplash-type telephone lines. It must be worrying that a man with his sort of background is not only now setting up what is allegedly a wholesome family newspaper but is also buying shares here, there and everywhere.'[7]

David Sullivan has become completely immune to such criticisms. He draws their sting by quoting from the slogans and mottoes he has collected over the years and which he now proudly displays in his office. One sign simply says 'Press On' while another advises 'Perseverance and Determination'. Sullivan places a lot of faith in these simple homilies and has done all he can to put them into practice.

John East remembers that on one occasion Sullivan even invented his own catchphrase. He says, 'David seems to work by slogans. Once he was very angry and pacing up and down his little office and I said, "Dave, what's the matter with you?" He said, "I think I'm off today, I'm not making as much money as I should. I've got to think of another slogan." I suggested "Think Big," but he said, "No, no, not Think Big. Think Huge. Do you know I'm the only businessman in this country who makes 1,000 per cent profit?"'

This is not necessarily an exaggeration. David Sullivan's extraordinary expectations had also been noticed by his staff at Sport Newspapers. Ian Pollack, a former *Sunday Sport* editor, worked closely with Sullivan for four years. He says that 'David wants to invest a hundred pounds and see a return of ten thousand. He wants instant returns and he wants it to be massive. It's his whole philosophy of life.'

Sullivan might want massive returns but, like many wealthy men, he is normally extremely careful with his money. John East recalled David Sullivan's look of approval when told of his meeting with Charlie Chaplin at the Savoy Hotel in London, where he had gone to record a radio broadcast. To East's astonishment, Chaplin, a millionaire many times over, was sitting in his hotel room stitching up a frayed cuff. Sullivan nodded in recognition of a like-minded man and touched the sleeve of his own jacket. 'I bought this suit off the peg,' he said proudly.

Until recently, David Sullivan's hobby was horse-racing and, according to Wetherby's, he was the largest resident owner of brood mares in Britain. He even toyed with the idea of buying 'lucky' Sandown racecourse. But, despite spending £300,000 a year running twenty-five racehorses, Sullivan didn't think that the sport's governing body ever gave him the respect he deserved. Finally, early in 1993, he angrily announced that he was getting out. 'Enough is enough,' he said. 'I've had eighteen years of being treated like a plonker.'[8]

Horse-racing's loss was to be football's gain. In March 1993 Sullivan revealed that he had bought Birmingham City Football Club from the receivers for £700,000. His first action was to authorize Terry Cooper, then manager of Birmingham City, to spend £500,000 in an attempt to move the club away from the relegation zone. Sullivan told the local paper that he had bought the club simply because 'I was attracted to the challenge. We are still schoolboys at heart and when you reach my age you can chase all those dreams you had as a boy.'[9]

But it is David Sullivan's private life that fascinates the public most of all. It has been the subject of numerous articles in the tabloid press and is almost impossible to exaggerate. Despite now wanting to project a more respectable image, Sullivan still described himself to *Tatler* magazine in April 1992 as a 'collector' of women and told a story which illustrated the point graphically. He said, 'I'm single and I'm naughty. Most guys like to think of themselves as collectors, me more than most. I had this problem once with the house in Chigwell when the toilet started playing up. I had to call Dyno-Rod. The whole plumbing system was blocked with thousands of condoms.'[10]

Tara Bardot, one of Sullivan's top models and a former girlfriend, thinks the description of him as a collector is absolutely accurate. Bardot confirms that he has an incredible number of sexual partners but says, 'He does it for the sake of it, not because he wants to. He really is like a collector. If a girl's willing to do it, he'll do it. He's just insatiable.'

Bardot recalls one night when she and Sullivan were planning to go out together. She was dressing when he decided that he wanted sex. Bardot declined the offer and so, unabashed, Sullivan hired a prostitute. She says, 'I remember I was getting ready and there was no way I was going to do it when I was getting ready because that would just spoil it. So he said, "Well, would you mind if I got somebody in then?" Anyway, he called this agency and this girl came along.' Bardot was more tolerant than many women might have been. She says, 'I didn't mind, he always uses a condom and anyway it got him off my back.'

Sullivan's use of escort agencies has become something of a joke to the journalists who have worked for him. He is apparently 'unavailable' between two and three o'clock in the afternoon, as Austin Mitchelson, the first editor of the *Sunday Sport*, quickly found out. 'You can get him in the morning but he has an "engagement" each afternoon and they won't put you through if you make a telephone call after two o'clock. I was told that two girls from an escort agency would arrive at the house and occupy him for an hour or so, five days a week.'

Despite his own promiscuity, Sullivan has always been surprisingly possessive about his girlfriends. Tara Bardot remembers there was always one rule for him and another for everyone else. 'He's allowed to see all the women he wants and bonk ten times a day. But he'd object if I were even talking to someone or he'd hear I was talking to someone. I'd say to him, "Well, look at how many women you bonk." And he'd say, "Yes, but I pay your bills."'

Sullivan often boasted to the newspapers that he had sex with every model who worked for him but, according to Bardot, this is actually a slight exaggeration. She points out that David Sullivan is no fool and says, 'If they're good enough, he'll give them a job anyway. But if they're not and they're willing to bonk him, he'd find them some work in one of the mags.'

But perhaps the most extraordinary sex claim made about David Sullivan, and there have been many, was that he once attempted to have sex with a thousand women in a single year. Sullivan told one of his newspaper editors that he had kept a careful note of each partner and was on target right up until the end of August when he was suddenly struck down by flu and out of action for several weeks. Despite what was described as a 'heroic' attempt to catch up in December, he finally missed his target by seven.

In the past, these sorts of stories have ensured continuing negative publicity for David Sullivan, but recently opinions have changed and the press has become far more ambivalent in its attitude towards him. This change has been brought about partly by Sullivan's own PR offensive, which he launched when he moved to Birch Hall, but also because of his claims that he has effectively abandoned the sex industry and is now primarily interested in newspaper publishing. Supporters like John East believe that the time has come for Sullivan to be reassessed. 'He's never been unethical to any person that I know. He's never been unjust to anybody. He's never employed hard or fighting characteristics. He says to me, "You've only got one life to lead, if they are nasty to me or they con me, you just turn around and walk away."'

But not everyone shares East's view of Sullivan as a much-maligned and misunderstood man. Rupert James works for the Rodox Corporation, the largest purveyors of pornography in the world. He has watched Sullivan closely for many years and seen his sharp business practices at first hand. James told *World in Action*, 'People sometimes have a cheap laugh at him but there is a lot of seriousness behind that cheap laugh. He uses the con man's maxim that there is a mug born every minute and I think he sleeps very well.'[11]

These two contradictory views sum up the puzzle that is at the heart of the David Sullivan story. Is he now one of Britain's leading businessmen, wrongly condemned because of events long ago? Or is he still, secretly, one of the major forces in Britain's sex industry, desperately trying to keep the cash it generates but hide its tainted source? This book will try to examine all the facts and then answer the one simple question: has Sullivan become the new prince of publishing or does he remain the sultan of sleaze?

NOTES

1. *Tatler*, April 1992.
2. *South Wales Echo*, 3 July 1993.
3. *Daily Mirror*, 4 April 1981.
4. *South Wales Echo*, 3 July 1993.
5. *World in Action*, Granada Television, 21 September 1992.
6. Ibid.
7. Ibid.
8. *Sunday Times*, April 1993.
9. *Birmingham Post*, 6 March 1993.
10. *Tatler*, April 1992.
11. *World in Action*, Granada Television, 21 September 1992.

CHAPTER TWO

BACHELORS OF SEX

David Sullivan was not always rich. Born on 5 February 1949, he lived with his parents and older brother, Clive, in a small semi-detached house in St David's Crescent, Penarth, which was part of a new council estate just outside Cardiff. Sullivan remembers his early years with real affection. 'Everyone had kids of the same age so there were hundreds of kids to play with. We used to play football, forty or fifty a side every night. And we used to fight the other estates and charge around – we had the most wonderful childhood.'[1]

David Sullivan believes that he learnt a lot from these formative years. 'We were quite poor, not starving, but we didn't have a car and at the end of the week there was no money left to buy anything. That makes you value money.'[2] It is a trait that has remained with him to this day. Despite becoming one of the wealthiest men in Britain, he refused to travel first class until a couple of years ago and only recently bought himself a really 'flash' car – a Bentley.

Sullivan's father was in the Royal Air Force and the whole family was uprooted several times as he was posted from base to base. They finished up at Hornchurch in Essex. Despite these interruptions to his education, Sullivan did remarkably well at school. His secondary education was provided first by Abbs Cross County Technical School and then by Watford Grammar School. He greatly impressed his teachers and his school reports were often glowing. In 1962 his form tutor wrote, 'David shows signs of leadership and the ability to organize . . . He is going to meet with great success if he continues in this vein.' Even the Headmaster became a fan, saying, 'I shall watch his future with interest.' They were not to be disappointed.

By the mid-sixties it was obvious to the young Sullivan that he was never going to achieve his ambition to be a professional sportsman (preferably a footballer or a heavyweight boxer). But what he lacked in physical prowess he more than made up for in mental agility. In 1967 his excellent 'A' level passes got him a place at London University's Queen Mary College where he studied for a degree in economics.

He must have been one of few students to arrive at Queen Mary College with a fully fledged business. Even at school Sullivan had been running a mail-order company buying and selling football magazines and souvenirs. 'I made a couple of thousand pounds,' he recalls, 'enough to buy a Ford Capri.' But a car was never going to satisfy Sullivan, as he freely admitted. 'I always wanted to be a millionaire.'[3]

His college friend and first business partner, Bernard Hardingham, vividly remembers the amount of football paraphernalia Sullivan kept at his home. 'He let me use the spare room and I was actually sleeping amongst all the football programmes.' Hardingham also remembers Sullivan's extraordinary drive. 'He was a very determined young man, keen to achieve academic success but mixing that with a business ability that had already made him reasonable sums of money.'

In 1969, David Sullivan won one of Queen Mary College's top academic awards. He became an Edward Stern Scholar, winning a £100 bursary in the process. But he is best remembered at the college for one particularly imaginative and significant fund-raising event. Sullivan had been appointed treasurer of the Economics Society only to discover that it was facing financial disaster. Immediate action was necessary to rectify the situation. Discos and dances had become commonplace – something extra was needed. The solution was classic David Sullivan. He hired topless go-go dancers to make sure the Queen Mary College Economics Society disco was a sellout. According to Bernard Hardingham, attendance was 'massive' and the Society's financial problems disappeared overnight.

Sullivan graduated in 1970 with a good 2.1 degree and started work with the Baron Moss advertising agency. They handled the Heron Group's promotional activities and one of Sullivan's more interesting assignments was to spend Saturday mornings touring petrol stations with Heron boss, Gerald Ronson. Hardingham believes that Gerald Ronson had a profound influence on Sullivan. 'I think he enjoyed actually being close to somebody who was a self-starter, had an eye for detail and just wouldn't finish the day until he attended to everything, just like David himself.' Much later, Ronson and Sullivan were to find they had something else in common: they both became Ford Open Prison old boys.

The friendship between Bernard Hardingham and David Sullivan became even stronger after college. They both moved into Hardingham's parents' home and were determined to set up their own business. 'We both knew there was no money and no future in working for anybody else,' says Hardingham. 'We had to cast around for different ideas.' Their first idea was a financial magazine which would utilize their college skills. It was to be called the *Investment Quarterly Journal* and would report on the financial scene for the wealthy personal investor. They prepared a rate card, asked a number of senior City figures to contribute articles and got a generally favourable reaction. But there was a problem. 'The trouble was,' recalls Hardingham, 'that neither David nor I were space salesmen and we didn't quite know how to take it forward.' Reluctantly, they decided to shelve the *Investment Quarterly*.

Sullivan then read the *News of the World* article that was to change his life. It profiled Bob Guccione, founder of *Penthouse* magazine and a man who had got rich by selling photographs of nude women through mail order. If Guccione could do it, reasoned Sullivan, why not me? Sullivan convinced Hardingham of the viability of his scheme and they pooled their entire savings of £200 to hire a photographer, four models and a studio just off Oxford Street. Eventually, twenty pictures of naked women in various explicit poses were printed on to one A3 sheet, and Sullivan and Hardingham were in business. Less than twelve months out of college, they had graduated from Bachelors of Science to Bachelors of Sex.

Sales of the photographs were initially slow despite Sullivan's detailed knowledge of the mail-order market gleaned from his days running the football programmes business. He placed adverts offering 'Twenty Nude Lovelies for a Pound' in everything from adult magazines like *Knave* and *Fiesta* to *Exchange & Mart* and *Titbits* (a publication Sullivan was later to buy and relaunch as a soft-porn magazine), but there were very few sales. As the cash began to run out, Sullivan and Hardingham held a crisis meeting to tackle the problem. 'We had to get back to basics and analyse why we weren't

getting the response and frankly our adverts weren't offering anything more than the competition,' recalls Hardingham. 'So we
decided to offer 200 pictures for a pound. The fact that it was ten
sheets the same may have disappointed some customers but nevertheless it certainly generated a tremendous response.'

Sullivan remembers the moment well. He told *Marketing Business*
magazine: 'I went from earning £1,700 a year to £800 a week.'[4] It
was the start of a rise that would eventually give him control of a
substantial part of the UK's sex industry as well as several national
newspapers.

Sullivan and Hardingham set up Subdean Publishing Ltd. to
control their embryonic, but potentially very lucrative, empire. By
mutual consent it was a shoe-string operation and all spare cash was
immediately reinvested in the business. Descriptions of the office
have varied from 'plain' to 'poky'. Subdean's activities quickly
expanded and soon embraced sex books, magazines and marital aids
as well as photographs. There was even a sex shop beneath the
office for personal callers. However the marketing strategy always
remained the same: promising much but delivering rather less.

It was a technique that impressed George Harrison Marks, a
legendary British pornographer in his own right who went on to
direct one of Sullivan's most famous sex films, *Come Play With Me*.
Harrison Marks remembers one particularly controversial advertisement offering pictures of women and dogs. 'Wow,' he says. 'That
was something in those days and obviously the mail was enormous.'
In fact, what Sullivan and Hardingham actually sent out was not
quite what the customers would have hoped for – but it was
perfectly legal. They supplied *Health & Efficiency* pictures of girls
playing tennis, with dogs in the background. George Harrison
Marks generously described it on *World in Action* as 'an honest con
trick'.[5]

Another Subdean trick involved buying old copies of *Health &
Efficiency*, *Knave* and *Fiesta* and printing explicit new front pages so
that the magazines appeared to be hard-core Scandinavian imports.
These were then resold at hugely inflated prices. George Harrison
Marks watched in amazement as the money flooded in. He couldn't
believe it. 'All the punters were getting was old stock served up in a
new cover.' Bernard Hardingham concedes that some customers

THE SULTAN OF SLEAZE

may have felt a little let down. 'I think there was some disappointment that it was not as strong as perhaps certain customers hoped for, but we were trying to keep within the bounds of the law at the time.' It may have been sharp practice but it quickly became very profitable. 'It was only after a few months when we started having our own books and magazines printed that we were able to achieve the mark-up we were really looking for,' recalls Bernard Hardingham. On occasions that mark-up reached 1,000 per cent.

The response to their advertisements also brought another bonus. Subdean Publishing quickly built up a mailing list of 60,000 customers, probably the most comprehensive list of porn buyers ever assembled in Britain. It cried out to be exploited and David Sullivan was the man to do so. From his dingy offices in Forest Gate, east London, Sullivan set up a sophisticated computerized mailshot operation. The people on the list were hit every ten days with new offers for sex books, magazines and films. The cash simply poured in. According to Bernard Hardingham, 'David was just totally relentless and once a customer had shown they wanted to buy our literature they were offered many opportunities. After all, not everybody wants to actually buy across the counter in a newsagent whereas a brown paper envelope coming through the post is quite acceptable.'

Within eighteen months of being set up, Subdean Publishing had taken a staggering 90 per cent of the UK sex mail-order market and, according to George Harrison Marks, had totally revolutionized the business. 'We were very complacent,' he says. 'Sullivan took outrageous chances and advertised outrageous things and it worked. We were all sick as dogs. He made a big impression.' But hard work was as important as hype to Subdean's success. 'David and I worked seven days a week,' recalls Hardingham. 'For five days a week we used to meet in the office between six and six-thirty in the morning and probably finish about seven or eight in the evening. Then we'd certainly work well into Saturday afternoon and most of Sunday. It takes a long time to stick 60,000 stamps on envelopes.'

Mail order was just the start for David Sullivan and Bernard Hardingham. Subdean now owned thousands of pictures of nude women and had a growing reputation in the market-place. For two economics graduates the next move was obvious – vertical integration. The company needed to launch its own sex magazine. Sullivan decided that the new magazine would be called *Private*, a name he 'borrowed' from a well-known continental sex chain, and would be sold in the shops, not through mail order. The man he brought in to produce it was universally known in the industry as Dirty Harry and was rightly famous for his skill and expertise in pornographic magazine production. Sullivan, however, kept overall control of the project for himself.

Sullivan installed Doreen Millington, a good-looking 23-year-old former sales representative from Stoke, as the first editor of *Private*. He has always believed that men find it more exciting if an attractive woman is supposedly running the operation, though their real responsibilities are not always clear. It's a technique he uses to this day, with glamour models Zeta Ross and Tara Bardot the nominal editors of *Parade* and *Titbits* respectively. The exact relationship between David Sullivan and Doreen Millington still remains a little mysterious, but he later named a blow-up doll after her and even persuaded an actress called Mary Maxted to adopt her surname: as Mary Millington she would become one of the most famous porn stars of all time.

The distribution of *Private* was to be carried out by Moore Harness, a company that would later figure prominently in Sullivan's life. In 1979 it was bought by Ralph Gold (one of the people behind the Ann Summers sex shops) and was eventually used to distribute both the *Daily Sport* and *Sunday Sport*. However, this was far in the future and, at this early stage, Sullivan was more worried about the company's level of commitment to *Private*. According to Bernard Hardingham, 'David decided, in his usual business style, that Moore Harness couldn't be left to handle it on their own and so he employed staff in-house to canvass newsagents up and down the country. They talked directly to the retailers in an effort to promote the new magazine.' But not even this was enough for the determined David Sullivan. He also took out full-page advertisments in some of the other soft-porn magazines, spending £50,000 giving 'Ten hard reasons why *Private* is the best value for money.'

Bernard Hardingham watched with admiration as his partner

launched their new magazine. 'David is the sort of person who, if a campaign didn't go well, would quite often become physically ill. That's his degree of commitment.' Fortunately, it wasn't necessary for Sullivan to become ill. *Private* soon became firmly established on the top shelf of Britain's newsagents.

As Subdean transformed itself from a small mail-order company to a major provider of pornography in Britain, the laws of economics began to assert themselves formidably. It became obvious that the direct-sales team should be pushing more than just one product and so Sullivan, driven by his own inexorable logic, began to launch magazine after magazine with names like *London Sex Guide*, *Blockbuster* and *Climax*. Each one tested the boundaries of acceptability just a little more.

Given the growing and increasingly explicit nature of Subdean's output plus the climate of the time – it was the early seventies and Mary Whitehouse and the Festival of Light were trying to spearhead a moral revival in Britain – it soon became inevitable that Sullivan and Hardingham would eventually come to the attention of the authorities. Their first confrontation with the police was a relatively low-key affair arising out of their mail-order operation. They were charged with sending indecent literature through the post (an offence under the Post Office Act). The matter was dealt with at the local Magistrates Court where they pleaded guilty and were fined. David Sullivan and Bernard Hardingham, while not pleased about the conviction, decided to regard it as an occupational hazard. According to Hardingham, 'The competition was reacting to our various offers and we had to try and push the threshold of acceptability forward.' What was of far greater concern to them was the growing possibility of a police raid on their warehouse which would not only leave them facing another set of charges but could close down their entire operation.

They decided to create a number of apparently separate mail-order companies, in the hope that this would reduce their profile, discourage potential rivals by suggesting the market-place was full and create the illusion for the customer that there was more choice available than was actually the case. In fact, the strategy comprehensively backfired on them. The police knew who were behind the new companies and became convinced that Sullivan and Hardingham were actually massively expanding their operations. They decided to mount a pre-emptive strike and launched a series of coordinated raids on all of Subdean's premises including the new ones. Sullivan and Hardingham were once again arrested but this time they faced the much more serious charges of publishing obscene material and conspiring to send obscene material through the post.

The situation was potentially very worrying for both of them, particularly bearing in mind their previous conviction. None the less they genuinely believed that the police had over-reacted and so demanded an old-style Section Two committal hearing. This meant the police were obliged to prove to a magistrate that there was a case to answer. While the hearing did reveal a number of weaknesses in the police case, these were not considered significant enough to allow for a dismissal. The proceedings were transferred to the Old Bailey.

The trial itself was something of a vindication for Sullivan and Hardingham. They pleaded guilty but claimed in mitigation that what was being sent in the post was 'contemporary literature'. They were each fined £50, a comparatively small sum, and the police were reprimanded for wasting the court's time.

But Sullivan and Hardingham had not just come to the attention of the police. Lord Longford was now preparing his famous report on pornography and asked to interview the two young graduates. The meeting, however, was not a success. Hardingham claimed that Longford seemed more interested in giving them fatherly advice about their choice of career than in hearing their views on pornography. His first question set the tone of the interview: 'It's rather a weird choice, isn't it? I don't know what your parents would think of it.' Hardingham, a little taken aback, replied that his parents would show a 'vague sort of unease' but at the end of the day would understand it was simply 'a business'. After asking some other questions about their mail-order activities Lord Longford tried again: 'You would agree with my account of these people that they are very sick?' David Sullivan most definitely did not agree and pointed out that their customers included landed gentry, clergymen, policemen and even the headmaster of a Roman Catholic school.

Afterwards, Sullivan claimed that the whole interview was a wasted opportunity and Lord Longford had made no effort to obtain any information from them that could have helped his report. He accused Lord Longford of showing 'a lack of professionalism' and told the *Daily Telegraph*, 'He didn't really want to see us. When we did see him the interview lasted only fifteen minutes. We thought we would be questioned by a panel but only Lord Longford was there. He seemed more concerned about a television appearance he was making that night than in what we had to tell him. He kept asking his secretary about it.'[6]

Away from the police and the nobility, Sullivan and Hardingham were doing better than ever. Sullivan had a luxurious penthouse apartment in Woodford, east London, expensively furnished with chrome, smoked glass and leather. Hardingham had a four-bedroom town house which was slightly more restrained but equally palatial. They had both acquired fast cars and were starting to become familiar faces on the London night-club scene. 'I think we drew £5,000 to £6,000 a year as salaries,' recalls Hardingham, 'and then we had the odd bonus. Our policy was absolutely scrupulous. We vigorously reinvested in the company, essentially to expand the business.'

This policy meant that Subdean Publishing was becoming increasingly profitable. The number of staff directly employed by the company had swelled to fifteen and the time had come to expand further. After months of negotiating, the *Sunday Times* finally agreed to allow Subdean to advertise in its pages. 'We were buying remaindered stock from Granada Publishing,' says Hardingham, 'legitimate stuff like antique books and *The History of English Frigates*. And we were then able to introduce things like the *ABC of Love*. It meant we could add to our mailing list those people who didn't have the courage to go into a sex shop.' Another new item on their list was a book entitled *We Made £200,000*, written by the bashfully modest David Sullivan and Bernard Hardingham. Now a collector's item, it chronicled their first three years in business and offered guidance to less successful entrepreneurs.

By the end of 1972, Sullivan and Hardingham had accumulated almost £300,000 in spare cash at the bank and their accountants were strongly advising them to invest their money. To this end they set up two property companies, Boufond Properties and Eurohols Properties. Boufond Properties concentrated on buying new or nearly new residential houses, mostly in the Forest Gate and Wood-ford areas of London. These properties were then furnished and let out, offering the prospect of both a reasonable income and some capital appreciation. Eurohols Properties concentrated on more speculative ventures, primarily buying properties occupied by sitting tenants in the hope that they could be persuaded to move and the property then resold at a higher price.

As the property boom of the early seventies increased so did Sullivan and Hardingham's exposure to the market. Not content with the two property companies making selective investments, they decided to gear up and use Subdean Publishing's enormous income stream to allow them to raise even larger mortgages and purchase really substantial properties, including several blocks of flats on the South coast. It was shortly to prove to be the most expensive mistake of their lives. The 1974 property crash was catastrophic for Sullivan and Hardingham. They had not only invested every penny they had made during the last three years in real estate but had also borrowed massively in a bid to transform themselves into property tycoons. Now they were facing disaster and feared they would lose everything.

The biggest hit was taken by their master company, Subdean Publishing. Price falls of up to 50 per cent meant that many of its properties were now worth no more than the mortgages they secured and some even had loans that were larger than the value of the buildings (a phenomenon that became known in the nineties as 'negative equity'). Eurohols Properties was in an equally desperate state. The maelstrom surrounding the property market made it virtually certain that no sitting tenant would want to move for the foreseeable future and this left the company looking at huge trading losses. Only Boufond Properties might have survived as it had moved more cautiously, carefully selecting its purchases and taking out relatively small loans. However, the enormous losses of its sister companies meant that it too would eventually have to be sacrificed.

Looking back, Hardingham believes that he and Sullivan spent too much time running the publishing company and not enough time supervising their investments. He says, 'We worked so hard with Subdean that we were totally dependent on the advice of others apart from the selected property purchases that we made on our own doorstep.' He calculates that '£300,000 of our money was written off.'

Incredibly, worse was still to come. Immediately after the property crash, Sullivan and Hardingham fell victims to an obscure tax law which was abolished just a few years later. Under this shortfall law, if the profits of a business were not reinvested in the principal activity of the business (in Subdean's case, magazine publishing) they were deemed to have been distributed as income to the directors and therefore attracted tax at the top rate of 83 per cent. Now the two young entrepreneurs faced an enormous tax bill on top of everything else.

But perhaps most galling of all was the fact that, just before the property market collapsed, they had seriously considered liquidating their investments and buying a headquarters building for Subdean. According to Hardingham, 'We'd actually discussed whether we should realize all our investments and buy ourselves a freehold property for our own use, which is absolutely ironic because that would have avoided the tax nightmare we were subsequently confronted with.'

The shortfall tax assessment was the *coup de grâce* for David Sullivan and Bernard Hardingham's first attempt to become multi-millionaires. The fruits of three years' hard work had disappeared overnight. Hardingham, who had become increasingly disillusioned with the sex industry and was about to be married, decided to get out altogether. David Sullivan, still very much a single man and a real fighter, decided to stay in and start again from scratch with a brand new company, Roldvale.

NOTES

1. *South Wales Echo*, 3 July 1993.
2. *Marketing Business*, October 1991.
3. *Guardian*, 16 June 1976.

4. *Marketing Business*, October 1991.
5. *World in Action*, 21 September 1992.
6. *Daily Telegraph*, 21 September 1992.

CHAPTER THREE

COME PLAY WITH ME

Roldvale Limited picked up the pieces after Subdean Publishing's crash. It was registered on 27 June 1975 and remains David Sullivan's master company to this day. It originally listed its business activities as magazine publishing, film production and racehorse breeding – Sullivan's new interest. Roldvale's first two directors were given as David Sullivan and Doreen Millington, the editor of *Private* magazine.

Despite managing to salvage the remnants of both the old Subdean business and the sex shop beneath his office, David Sullivan was still in serious financial trouble. He desperately needed a new cash generator and so he decided to launch his most explicit sex magazine yet, the 'bra bustin', spread-legged' *Whitehouse*, provocatively named after Mrs Mary Whitehouse, the self-appointed guardian of the nation's morals. Not surprisingly a massive row erupted – as Sullivan had intended all along. The free publicity soon had its desired effect and *Whitehouse* became one of the best-selling adult magazines.

Sullivan began to revel in the publicity his stunts generated. He called his next magazine *Ladybirds*. This time the children's book publishers, Ladybird, were the victims and they eventually decided to go to court to protect their name. Sullivan was forced to back down, again in a blaze of free publicity, and renamed his now infamous periodical *Playbirds*. Another publicity stunt pioneered by Sullivan came from his growing love of horse-racing. Sullivan realized that you can't advertise sexual material on television but you can race horses and so he started to name his growing stable after his magazines. It wasn't long before *Playbirds* and later *Miss Park Lane* were embarrassing the commentators as they thundered round the racecourses of Britain.

David Sullivan's controversial methods were quickly turning him into one of the most infamous young men in Britain. It was at this point that he came to the attention of John East, the BBC radio broadcaster. East is now a firm friend of Sullivan and even took part in a number of Sullivan's sex films but he still vividly recalls their first meeting. 'I was doing a radio series on entrepreneurs and I heard of a guy called David Sullivan who was running a sex shop in the East End of London. I went down there to a tacky little shop in Forest Gate and up these rickety stairs and there was this round, aggressive little guy who said, "What do you want and how long are you going to take?" I could see he was very sharp and very shrewd and he knew exactly what he wanted. I was going to give him this broadcast and he thought that would bring plenty of punters into the shop and it was therefore worth five minutes of his time.'

Soon this 'round, aggressive little guy' and his provocative products would become even more well known. By the mid-seventies his sex magazines were selling almost a million copies a month. This success was not due solely to Sullivan's nose for publicity but also to the way he had substantially modified his marketing techniques. He recognized that most of his magazines were now being sold in shops and this meant reducing the extravagant claims. After all, shopkeepers might decide that it was too risky to stock the magazines if they purported to be hard-core pornography. It also meant that the customers could compare and contrast the various products before buying. Sullivan realized that he was now in a genuine market-place and decided that the best way to win was to compete aggressively on price. John East watched it happen. 'Before David Sullivan really came on the scene there were plenty of glamour magazines. But his magazines were half the cost and he gave two for the price of one.'

There was probably a third reason for the success of Sullivan's magazines. They did not feature models who were so beautiful that they were obviously beyond the reach of the readership. The girls were attractive but they looked as though they could be found in any British town. The models in most of his competitors' magazines looked as though they could only be found in Hollywood.

This idea that girls could be too attractive found its highest form in another Sullivan innovation, 'Readers' Wives'. Sullivan started publishing explicit pictures of amateur models which had been sent in to his magazines by the readers. Not only did they cost virtually nothing to print but they also became one of the most popular features. John East puts this genuine insight into the customers' preferences down to Sullivan's background. 'The key to David Sullivan is that he came from a lower-middle-class background and he understands the processes of a young working man's mind. You see, he's no Robert Redford or Steve McQueen, and he realized that a lot of fellows couldn't get girls in night-clubs or bars and the alternative was to buy a magazine and fantasize over it. His magazines were designed for working-class people.'

George Harrison Marks had also noted Sullivan's skill in identifying gaps in the market that found favour with the buying public. 'They bought it and they came back for more. Obviously it appealed to them. He drew a particular market, he knew what that particular public wanted and it was a large percentage of the public.'

However, not all of Sullivan's publications were as successful as his sex magazines. In 1976 he tried to launch a newspaper that, in retrospect, was clearly the forerunner of the *Sunday Sport*. It was called *Private National News*. In an interview with the *Guardian* Sullivan described it as 'a sex-scandal newspaper in magazine format' and he went on to outline his idea in some detail. 'There have been several of these papers in Britain before but they all failed because you can't display them on the counter. Some people even say it's wrong to have the *Sun* on the counter. This will have a clean front cover, no stronger than a tube advert, with a warning on the front saying "adults only". We'll investigate actresses, models, popstars, businessmen and politicians. In the first issue we expose well-known models who are working as prostitutes on the side. We criticize them not for being prostitutes but for operating from council flats. That, to me, is very anti-social. If you earn £1,000 a week why should you be subsidized by taxpayers?'[1]

Sullivan planned to get his material from tabloid journalists whose editors had spiked their stories. 'We've got Sunday newspaper reporters who will give us stuff their papers can't print,' and, he added pointedly, 'Being in the business, you do hear an awful lot.'[2] Despite his confidence, *Private National News* was not a success and Sullivan had to wait until 1986 and the launch of *Sunday Sport* before he finally got a national newspaper.

David Sullivan's other big 1976 foray was his move into film production. George Harrison Marks finally persuaded him of its virtues but, like most things Sullivan did, it also had its own internal logic. After all, Sullivan reasoned, the film could be promoted in the magazines and there was no shortage of girls willing to take part.

George Harrison Marks had already made three feature-length sex films, *The Naked World of Harrison Marks*, *The Nine Ages of Nakedness* and *Naked as Nature Intended* (which had the dubious distinction of being the first film to show a completely naked woman on the British cinema screen). He was looking for a backer for his latest project, *Come Play With Me*, when David Sullivan suddenly turned up on his doorstep.

'Dave came along to buy some pictures and for the first time he sat down and had a cup of tea. We got talking and he said, "Why aren't you making any more feature films?" I said, "I've got a great film script. It's about a bunch of girls who were strippers in Paris and come over here. I'm looking for someone with lots of money to finance it." He thought it sounded great and said, "What sort of money would that cost to make?" So I told him £100,000 which was really very low budget.' Less than a week later George Harrison Marks got his backer. David Sullivan's master company, Roldvale, agreed to finance fully *Come Play With Me*. It would feature a number of fine comedy actors but a condition was that it had to star David Sullivan's girlfriend, Mary Millington.

Mary Millington's appearances in Sullivan's sex films would eventually turn her into Britain's first genuine sex queen. Born Mary Quilter, she was the illegitimate daughter of an opera critic and a civil servant. She grew up in Fulham and, at the age of eighteen, married Robert Maxted. She began working as a fashion model but quickly switched to nude work. Despite not being conventionally beautiful, the camera liked her and she positively enjoyed showing off her body, as some of her films demonstrate. Mary took Doreen Millington's surname when she began working for David Sullivan and eventually replaced Doreen as editor of *Whitehouse* magazine.

John East recalls how David Sullivan spotted Mary's potential early on and decided to invest heavily in her. 'David analysed her and said, "Your teeth are wrong, your nose is wrong. We'll get your teeth fixed, we'll have your nose reshaped and then you'll get more work as a model."' The cosmetic surgery financed by Sullivan certainly paid off and, thanks to some outrageous publicity stunts including posing topless outside the Houses of Parliament and 10 Downing Street, Millington went on to become an international sensation.

David Sullivan's decision to feature Mary in *Come Play With Me* was part of a deliberate strategy to change her from a model to a star and this probably explains Sullivan's decision to finance the film in the first place. It is a technique that he's tried to repeat with almost all of his leading models, including Julie Lee, Zeta Ross, Tara Bardot and Trine Michelson, but it has really only worked with Mary Millington.

Come Play With Me has been called a 'Carry On' film with sex scenes added. The plot is ridiculously simple. It involves two counterfeiters, played by director George Harrison Marks and Alfie Bass, stealing some Bank of England printing plates and then hiding in a old stately home owned by Irene Handl. Unbeknown to them, the house has been transformed into an exclusive health clinic now populated by lots of sexy young nurses who provide much more than just medical check-ups. Mary Millington has a relatively small part as one of the nurses, though she features in several of the film's sexier scenes including one where she shares an intimate moment with another nurse on an exercise bed. Many so-called 'connoisseurs' of porn claim that this scene has some added value since Millington was openly bisexual and may not have been acting at the time that this lesbian sex scene was shot.

David Sullivan went to quite exceptional lengths to ensure the success of *Come Play With Me*. Using his well-tried method for obtaining publicity, he controversially told the press that 'The sex scenes will make Linda Lovelace look like Noddy. They show the lot. Nothing is simulated.'[3] In fact, despite Mary Millington's best efforts, it was really quite a tame affair.

Sullivan's comments undoubtedly helped to publicize the film but they made George Harrison Marks's job as director very difficult indeed. 'David kept on putting out these terrible stories that we were making two versions – including a porn version – and I had some of the best names in comedy there. I got such flak from the technicians' union and Equity.' Equity, the actors' union, stepped in because some of the more well-known performers involved, like Alfie Bass, Irene Handl and Ronnie Fraser, had contacted them fearing that more sex scenes were being added. The row quickly assumed epic proportions and became front-page news, as Sullivan had always intended. Carl Snitcher, Equity's assistant general secretary at the time and now Paul Raymond's legal adviser, told the *Daily Telegraph*, 'We have heard on the grapevine that a continental version of *Come Play With Me* is being prepared and that pornographic scenes have been inserted into it. The main actors are unaware that this has been going on and we think their reputations could be damaged by their unwitting involvement in a film of this kind.'[4] In fact, no foreign version exists – it was all just part of the hype orchestrated by Sullivan.

This artificial controversy guaranteed that *Come Play With Me* would become a huge hit. It played to packed houses right across the country and was not only popular but extremely profitable as well. It had cost just £83,000 to make and eventually grossed over £3 million. David Sullivan's Roldvale company owned 75 per cent and George Harrison Marks the other 25 per cent; but that situation was not to last.

Once a month George Harrison Marks travelled to Sullivan's east-London offices to collect his part of the proceeds. Each month they discussed how much longer the film would run and each time Harrison Marks became a little gloomier about its future prospects. One afternoon the teetotal Sullivan suddenly produced a bottle of Scotch and the discussion turned to the possibility of a buy-out. George Harrison Marks told *World in Action* what happened next. 'I said, "Dave, give me twenty grand and you can have my 25 per cent." He said, "You've got to be joking." So we bickered and it came down to about fifteen grand. The bottle of Scotch had been going down and I said, "If you can put fifteen grand on the table in cash right now we'll do a deal." Well, within fifteen minutes there was fifteen grand on the table and I did the deal.' It was a deal that George Harrison Marks regretted the minute he sobered up, as he sadly remembers. 'It was a beautiful deal for him. The bloody thing ran for another three years.'[5]

The financial success of *Come Play With Me* surprised even David Sullivan and he became an enthusiastic backer of British sex films.

He even stopped describing himself as a 'magazine publisher' in some Companies House documents and switched to the more glamorous sobriquet, 'film producer'. Sullivan's other films included *Playbirds* (named after his magazine) and *The David Galaxy Affair*, but none of them was as well received or as financially successful as *Come Play With Me*.

Playbirds starred Mary Millington, who played an undercover policewoman given the task of finding a maniac killer. Her co-star was Alan Lake, the husband of Diana Dors. He was a particularly erratic and violent man who some believe was responsible for introducing Millington to the drugs and the dangerous lifestyle that would eventually lead to her death. The film's supporting cast included Windsor Davies, Glyn Edwards and Gavin Campbell, who later joined *That's Life*.

Ten years later, Campbell's involvement in *Playbirds* was hypocritically exposed by the *Sunday Sport* in a front-page lead headlined '*That's Life* Star in Sex Video'. According to the *Sunday Sport*, 'TV's Esther Rantzen learns today that another of her boys has been up to hanky panky. *That's Life* presenter Gavin Campbell stars in a naughty blue video. He really gives it stick in *Playbirds*.'[6] The article then went on to describe some of the film's more lurid scenes. However, the *Sunday Sport*'s front page somehow managed to avoid the fact that Campbell actually only had a straight supporting role in the film, which had in fact been produced by their publisher, David Sullivan, who had just reissued it on video.

Sullivan's next film, *The David Galaxy Affair*, was released in 1979 and supposedly contains some autobiographical elements – the plot involves a pornographer suffering police harassment. At the time of production both Sullivan and Mary Millington were facing charges of publishing an obscene edition of *Whitehouse* magazine, though they were later acquitted. After the court case, Millington wrote in her diary, 'How can it be pornographic to show people doing what comes so naturally? I've been making sex films since I was a young girl and I've never felt degraded.'[7]

The pressure that Millington felt herself to be under didn't prevent her from steadily improving as an actress. She was coached for her last film by broadcaster John East, who also co-starred, though he wisely decided to keep his clothes on. The film was called *Queen of the Blues* and was shot in the Burlesque night-club in Soho. Millington played a stripper whose successful act ensured the survival of the club, which was threatened by local thugs. The film eventually ran for thirty-eight weeks at the Eros in Piccadilly and comfortably covered its costs.

By now the relationship between David Sullivan and Mary Millington had become very close indeed, but the strain caused by her high profile in the sex industry was starting to tell. Millington's behaviour became increasingly erratic. She became obsessed with money. On a promotional tour for *Come Play With Me* she blatantly worked as a high-class call girl. She even started shoplifting. East, Millington's mentor and friend, looked on but was powerless to stop the decline.

'Mary was under tremendous pressure,' he recalls. 'She mixed with bad company, she was introduced to drugs and she was introduced to other unpleasant practices. I saw her deteriorating and I was fond of this funny little girl who saw me as a sort of father confessor. I said, "What makes you steal, Mary, what's the motivation?" She said, "It's purely a thrill – I'll show you." We were walking through the West End and there was a shop with a lighted window and inside was a dining-room display. She said, "I'm going to nick that lamp from the dining room," and I said, "My God, well I'm not going in the shop." So I stood there and Mary Millington, at peak time, went into the shop, went into the window, took the lamp from the table and walked out.'

David Sullivan, too, had become increasingly concerned about his girlfriend's erratic behaviour. In an effort to give her life some stability he helped her set up two sex shops of her own, one in Tooting called 'The Mary Millington Magazine Centre' and the other in Norbury. She certainly enjoyed her new job, telling John East that the most thrilling part of all was 'cashing up at the end of the day'.

But even the challenge of running two sex shops did not calm her down. After shooting *The David Galaxy Affair*, Mary Millington made several genuinely hard-core films which she openly sold in her shops. She also got into considerable difficulties with the Inland Revenue over her tax affairs. These factors, coupled with her drug taking, shoplifting and generally wild lifestyle, meant that the authorities were never going to leave her alone. She was arrested three times in the first seven months of 1979.

On 19 August that year Mary Millington committed suicide at her home in Epsom by taking an overdose of sleeping pills. She was thirty-three years old. In a note to her solicitor she revealed much of her anguish: 'I never liked people, only animals . . . the police killed me with threats . . . pornography will be legal here one day as it is in most countries but the abuse I receive from the police is unbearable. I am a kleptomaniac but try so hard to control my illness. I can't go on any longer. The police have threatened me so much. I can't face the thought of Holloway where they are determined to put me.'

David Sullivan had split up with Mary Millington just before her death but he was shocked by her suicide. He told the *Sunday Times* magazine, 'She always said, "I'll never grow old." She even trained to be a mortician, the last years of her life. After we broke up, we had a few shops together and a bit of a conflict about how the business should be run. She wanted to sell out-and-out porn but I said, "Take a little less money, have a little less hassle." But when she died I cried for a fortnight. I nearly had a kid with her and I regret that because if she'd had a kid she'd still be here today.'[8] John East also remembers just how upset Sullivan was by the tragedy. 'He was absolutely devastated. Not because he'd lost a good commercial operation in Mary Millington but out of a sense of personal loss.'[9]

None the less the death did not blunt Sullivan's commercial instincts. Within a few days of Mary Millington's death, Sullivan had commissioned a quickie 'tribute' film which seemed more about exploitation than about commemoration. The film, called *True Blue Confessions*, was shot at Millington's home. One scene was considered particularly offensive by her friends. It was filmed in her bedroom and pills had been scattered on the bed. The camera panned off the pills, past her suicide note, to a Millington lookalike lying semi-naked in a coffin. Even hardened professionals like George Harrison Marks felt that David Sullivan had gone too far this time. He said, 'Most of us who worked with her were terribly saddened by what happened and starting to see all this stuff was not on. They got hold of a girl who looked much like her and had her lying in a coffin which was a bit sick. Not a bit sick, very sick.'[10]

But Sullivan was unrepentant. He followed up the film with a 'tribute' record to Millington. The disc, which was described as 'a totally hot sexual experience', was offered to readers of *Whitehouse* magazine and began with the words 'Hello, this is Mary Millington.' It then went on to tell the story of a sexy weekend. Diana Dors, who had been one of Millington's many lesbian lovers, told the *News of the World*, 'I know her voice and the one on the record isn't it. It's a very poor imitation. I knew Mary for three years and was very fond of her. I think it's appalling and ghoulish they should be making money out of a dead person this way.'[11]

Doreen Millington, from whom Mary had taken her name and who had ceased working for David Sullivan two years earlier, also condemned the record, saying, 'This is disgusting exploitation.' But she went even further in attacking her former boss claiming that, 'A short time before Mary died she phoned me and told me David was trying to get rid of her. She said he told her she couldn't act. She was broken hearted. She'd always hated herself because of the life she led. I'm out of the business now and Mary is dead. But David is still making plenty of money out of the Millington name.'[12]

Sullivan, despite all the criticisms, has steadfastly maintained that both the film and the record were not exploitative in any way but were intended simply as tributes to Mary's memory. He later released another film using Millington's name, *Mary Millington's World Striptease Extravaganza*, but strangely this provoked little negative comment.

Millington's untimely death left Sullivan with a problem. He no longer had a leading lady for his films and he spent months searching for a suitable replacement. He wanted someone he could groom to be a star in much the same way that he had groomed Millington. Eventually he settled on Julie Lee, a strikingly beautiful woman of Chinese extraction, and she took the lead in his next film, *Emmanuelle in Soho*. He told John East, 'She's exotic. She'll pose for the magazines. She's a package I can use.' But Sullivan had overlooked one thing. According to East, 'She couldn't act. We had to make sure all her scenes were kept really short.'

There was also a growing problem with the British Board of Film Censors. They were becoming increasingly concerned about Sullivan's films and carefully studied *Emmanuelle in Soho*. East, who produced it, remembers one part of the ensuing row. 'I thought it would be rather nice if, at the finish, we had one of the girls bend over and we ended on her bum. But the BBFC said, "Oh no, you can see her fanny." You'd have to have a magnifying glass to see her fanny. They were just out to get us.'

The attentions of the British Board of Film Censors put David Sullivan in a very difficult position. His promotional material suggested that *Emmanuelle in Soho* was a hot and steamy sex film (which it had never been) but the cuts imposed by the BBFC diluted it even further. Sullivan now found himself in the ridiculous position of being challenged by Westminster's Trading Standards Officers because the film wasn't blue enough. Alan Sharpe, the officer in charge, told the press, 'The film itself is very tame. The adverts make it out to be more hard-core than it really is. They show photographs of steamy sex scenes with actors and actresses who aren't even in the film.' Sharpe said that his department was considering bringing proceedings as it felt the film's advertising misled the public.

Despite all these problems, *Emmanuelle in Soho* was a success and Julie Lee soon proved herself to be as adept as Mary Millington had been in getting publicity. She even agreed to marry a wealthy Egyptian businessman in exchange for him paying her £1 million. The deal was signed at the Concordia restaurant in Lancaster Gate and the story was splashed in the *Sunday Mirror*. David Sullivan appeared to have found another winner. Then, incredibly, tragedy struck again. In May 1983 Julie Lee was killed in a car crash on the way to a Maidenhead night-club.

Following Lee's death, Sullivan moved out of the mainstream soft-porn film market and into 'B' film production. He had decided that the costs of full-scale feature film production were no longer justified by the returns. He told John East, 'The revenue for feature pictures like *Emmanuelle in Soho* and *Queen of the Blues* isn't really worth it. Let's go for cheaper pictures that we can shoot in a day. It doesn't matter what it is. I can still hype it.'

The first of these low-budget films was called *Hellcat Mud Wrestlers* and was made in a deserted Croydon night-club for just £24,000. It starred a team of American female mud wrestlers who took on Sullivan's 'Roldvale girls'. The Americans were professional mud wrestlers led by Queen Kong, an enormous woman weighing over twenty-four stone who had previously wrestled with defanged bears. The Roldvale girls were simply Sullivan models and, not surprisingly, they lost the contest, though it's unlikely that anyone was watching for its sporting value. David Sullivan filmed three bouts and intercut it with full frontal interviews with the Roldvale girls and comments from the two managers. *Hellcat Mud Wrestlers* ran at some London cinemas as the support feature to Charles Bronson's *The Evil Men Do*, but is claimed to have been the bigger attraction of the two.

Sullivan's final film was called *Female Foxy Boxers* and again featured Queen Kong and the American mud wrestlers taking on the Roldvale girls, this time in the boxing ring. As before, the three-fight formula was used, but Sullivan insisted that at least one of the bouts was shot with the girls boxing topless. This was too much for the British Board of Film Censors who felt that the mixture of sex and violence was unacceptable. They refused to issue a certificate until the topless scene was cut from the film.

Their decision left Sullivan with a major problem. 'B' films had to run for a minimum of forty-five minutes and this one was now seven minutes short. Eventually he decided to combine *Hellcat Mud Wrestlers* with *Female Foxy Boxers* and reissue it as *Queen Kong, the Amazonian Woman*. It was released at the Moulin Complex in London's Soho and again easily covered its costs.

David Sullivan's interest in film production had been steadily declining since the late seventies but his decision to quit altogether was caused by the government's announcement that it was scrapping the Eady Levy. This was a grant that had previously been available to anybody who shot a film in Britain using a British film crew and its disappearance led to the virtual collapse of the British film industry. David Sullivan's *Female Foxy Boxers* may well have been the last 'B' film made in Britain, a strange end for a once-great industry.

NOTES

1. *Guardian*, 16 June 1976.
2. Ibid.

3. *News of the World*, 13 November 1976.
4. *Daily Telegraph*, 14 November 1976.
5. *World in Action*, 21 September 1992.
6. *Sunday Sport*, 26 July 1987.
7. *Sunday Sport*, 5 July 1987.
8. *Sunday Times*, 7 September 1986.
9. *World in Action*, 21 September 1992.
10. Ibid.
11. *News of the World*, 15 June 1980.
12. Ibid.

CHAPTER FOUR

VERY PRIVATE SHOPS

In 1978 David Sullivan made the most controversial move of his career so far. He decided to set up a chain of sex shops across Britain, trading under the 'Private Shop' banner. No one had tried to take sex to suburbia before and this bold move was to change both the face of the British sex industry and many British high streets for ever.

Once again, the economic logic behind his decision was inescapable. Sullivan already knew that there was strong consumer demand for his products and he could easily identify the best retail locations from the mail-order lists he had assembled over the previous eight years. He brought in his brother, Clive (who curiously preferred to be known as Frank), to supervise the project. Clive outlined their retail strategy on London Weekend Television's *London Programme*: 'If you have an area where you have very great demand on a mail-order basis, but with people saying "I would prefer to come and purchase personally rather than use mail order with all the subsequent delays," then under those circumstances that could lead us to open a shop.'[1]

The Private Shops were not to be controlled directly by Roldvale, David Sullivan's master company, but by a wholly owned subsidiary called Conegate which was first registered on 9 September 1978. In time Conegate was to become even more controversial than Roldvale, and Sullivan, weary of his never-ending battles with the authorities, appointed two of his senior managers – Brian Richards and David Reed – as Conegate's directors. The criticism inevitably generated by the company could now be taken by them. The final member of the management team that would lead Conegate's assault on Britain's high streets was Christine King, Sullivan's former secretary and now his very able administrator.

The first Private Shop was, predictably, opened in Soho, London's premier red-light district, and it set the tone for all the others. The windows were boarded up, everything was painted black, and the words 'Private Shop' were emblazoned in gold letters along the top. Stern warnings were put on the door that obscene material was on sale inside and that no one easily offended or under eighteen should enter the premises. As with all Sullivan businesses, frills were kept to an absolute minimum, but a full range of sex products was stocked ranging from magazines and films (mostly produced by Roldvale) to sex dolls, vibrators and lingerie (bought in from outside suppliers). The shop did not look incongruous in Soho, but it was designed for suburbia and the reactions there would be very different indeed.

The Private Shop chain expanded across the country at a tremendous rate, provoking hostility and opposition wherever it went. The reaction in Tunbridge Wells, Kent, was typical: the old spa town represents the very essence of middle-class respectability and many of its citizens were genuinely outraged at the prospect of a sex shop in their midst. Local churches led a vigorous campaign against the shop. The Reverend John Hurst, the vicar of St Peter's, was their spokesman. He claimed that the shop was unchristian and that it objectified women: 'I believe the sex shops and similar things are really destructive of family life. I also think they're a threat to womanhood. They treat a woman as an object, almost like a plastic throw-away cup, when they've finished they throw it away and get another. This is the kind of lifestyle that's presented and to many, many Christian people this kind of attitude to sex is a threat, undermining marriage principles and the Christian gospel.'[2]

It was not just clerics who were opposed to the Tunbridge Wells Private Shop. Many ordinary people were also prepared to speak out. They were particularly concerned that it was located in such a prominent place, situated on the main road between the central station and the post office. Pensioner Mrs Kathleen Davey was one of a number who said it scared them: 'I have to pass the sex shop in Vale Road to go and get my pension and I think it looks sinister. I don't know what's behind the dark windows but I'm quite sure it encourages undesirable people to come into this part of the town.'[3]

The local newspaper, the *Kent & Sussex Courier*, joined in the debate by running an opinion poll on the subject. Quentin Lloyd, the assistant editor, was in no doubt about the mood in Tunbridge Wells: 'Public opinion in the town has been running high since the sex shop opened and we conducted our own survey giving people the chance to say whether or not they favoured a sex shop here. The replies to this have shown overwhelmingly a "No". Something like 97 per cent of one thousand entries.'[4]

But the negative public reaction was not just found in the middle-class home counties. Conegate also encountered protests in the inner cities. The Private Shop in London's Tottenham High Road was besieged every Saturday for months by feminists and community groups. Reg Race, the local MP, helped organize a petition against it: 'People now understand that you can't have a large-scale pornography industry which portrays women in that kind of way and have a decent, liberated attitude towards women and their position in society. The two are quite incompatible.'[5]

The campaign against the setting up of the Private Shops in Britain's towns and villages crossed conventional political boundaries. Hard left and feminist organizations stood shoulder-to-shoulder with moral crusaders like Mary Whitehouse, who believed that one of the biggest dangers posed by sex shops was their negative effects on the young. 'When people go in those shops to buy things, they don't leave them behind,' she said, 'and you can get the kind of circumstances that we've had parents write to us about time and time again. Their children, whether they've been on playing fields or public parks or even in the streets, have picked up pages of magazines sold in these shops. The trouble is you cannot contain these things within the shops.'[6]

But the enormous negative reaction from some parts of the community didn't worry David Sullivan, the master publicist. He knew from past experience that sales always increased in direct proportion to the amount of protest encountered. It was a lesson that was soon learned by his employees.

Paul Price is a large and likeable man who now works as a private investigator but was previously employed by Conegate as an area manager. Price joined the company relatively early on and supervised the opening of a number of Private Shops in the South of England. He saw the hostile public reaction at first hand and Conegate's very interesting response to it: 'More or less every shop that opened either had faeces and paint thrown at it or a stream of local councillors, churchmen, vicars, nuns and orphans demonstrating against it saying how evil it was – it was pornography to the nth degree, brothels would be opened in the town, children would be abused, all that sort of rubbish. But the company loved it because it gave them free publicity and it meant everyone knew where the shops were when they opened.' Price remembers the opening of one shop particularly well. It was in Ryde on the Isle of Wight. 'I went over to the island a few days before the completion of the contract. There had been a tip-off as to what was opening up and one do-gooder was already up in arms with a petition trying to shut the shop before it had even opened. This was attracting the largest possible attention and I was interviewed in newspapers, on radio and television, all sorts of things. It was great free advertising.'

One of Paul Price's colleagues at the time was Martin Kennard. Now running a South-coast amusement arcade, he was once a Private Shop senior manager. He, too, recalls the vigorous campaign of opposition to the sex shops and Conegate's relaxed attitude towards it. 'There was an exceptional amount of local protest. There was a group of people that considered us immoral, illegal or whatever you care to say. But the company's attitude was pretty straightforward. This was the biggest free advertising there was. Everything they were doing out there, raging and shouting, made the local newspapers and television. It was great, it was free advertising.'

While the protesters may have considered the issues raised to be deadly serious, the Conegate staff did not always respond in kind. Shop managers up and down the country started telling reporters they were called John Holmes. Bemused journalists, not quite sure of the gag, went along with it and Mr Holmes became a familiar figure in the press, putting forward the sex shops' point of view. Only several years later did the press finally realize that the real John Holmes was in fact a particularly well-endowed actor who played the stud in many of Conegate's more pornographic videos.

One of the things that impressed people most about the early Conegate operation was the speed with which the shops were opened. Once Eamonn Connolly, David Sullivan's property manager, had identified and purchased a site things happened much faster than most local people anticipated. According to Paul Price,

'They used the same team to buy the premises, to equip them, to fill the shelves and open the shops. It only took a matter of days.' Martin Kennard remembers how frequently Conegate caught their opponents napping: 'They weren't ready for it, they didn't know what the hell was happening. They were hit with a very efficient machine that was selling sex. All of a sudden the "Private Shop" name came up, the windows got blacked out and bang, there was a sex-shop industry in your town.'[7]

And Conegate knew its market well. For every protester ready to shut the shop there was also a customer waiting to enter, as Kennard recalls: 'When a shop first opened it made a lot of money purely and simply because of the initial interest. People wanted to see what a sex shop was like. Sex shops are synonymous with Soho and everyone knows about Soho, that it's a dark and dangerous sort of place. All of a sudden you've got a little bit of Soho in your home town. It was daring and naughty and people were curious to see what was going on inside those blanked-out shops.'

Conegate's blitzkrieg tactics had been worked out in some detail by David Sullivan and his senior management. They virtually guaranteed the success of the Private Shop offensive. The protesters were sufficiently alert to draw attention to the shops but were rarely well organized enough to force the company to withdraw.

Sullivan's decision to take sex shops into the provinces was proving to be a masterstroke. It had not been done before on any significant scale and most of the towns represented virgin territory, as John East observed: 'He didn't have any rivals because there was no other person in the game. There were no other sex shops around, apart from Ann Summers, so there was virtually no competition. The success of any businessman is to find a hole in the market and expand rapidly. That was the success of David Sullivan.'

But even Sullivan made mistakes. On one occasion he agreed to get out of town in exchange for suitable compensation. It happened in St Helens, where he had just purchased a shop for £15,500 and begun the process of conversion. The usual string of protests followed and then, out of the blue, the Merseyside Community Standards Association offered to buy the property from him for £20,000, providing that Sullivan agreed not to set up another Private Shop within five miles of the site. The man who did the deal was Charles Oxley, the chairman of the MCSA and a well-respected local figure. He believes that the town had little choice but to try and buy off David Sullivan. 'I have no regrets over the St Helens deal. You could say £4,500 was a bribe or a pay-off but it was worth it if it prevented one girl getting raped. I believe these shops increase the number of sexual assaults.'[8] Sullivan took the £4,500 pay-off and immediately regretted it. He told the *News of the World*, 'I was soft. I talked to this nice Christian gent and let him persuade me. I could have earned up to £50,000 a year from that site. By the time I'd paid for the cancelled advertising and the manager I took on, I only had a few hundred pounds left.'[9]

It was a tactic which the MCSA tried to repeat at nearby Southport but this time Sullivan said he wanted to make at least £20,000 profit, a figure that shocked Oxley at the time. 'We couldn't raise that sort of money. We had a big protest meeting in Southport, attended by 1,200 people, and we collected £500, but it seems we cannot stop Sullivan opening his wretched shop.'[10]

David Sullivan was unperturbed by all the criticisms. 'I won't make the same mistake again,' he said. 'St Helens was a marvellous spot because there isn't another sex shop for miles. I could have made a fortune. But I listened to these protesters and let myself be persuaded. Afterwards hundreds of people wrote to me saying how disappointed they were that I changed my mind. My shops do a public service. We help people with their sex lives.'[11]

The Private Shops soon became one of the most profitable parts of the Sullivan empire. Conegate, in its first full year of operation, reported a profit of £849,303 and Brian Richards, the retail director, wrote in the directors' report, 'The company is trading successfully and now owns several freehold and leasehold properties from where it carries out its retail operations. It is vigorously continuing its expansion policies by acquiring additional trading premises throughout the United Kingdom.' Most of the Private Shop premises appear to have been bought outright for cash. Inspection of Conegate's accounts suggests that almost none of the shops have been mortgaged, which goes some way to explaining their extraordinary profitability. But there are a number of other factors that make the Private Shop operation virtually unique in Britain.

One element is the extraordinarily high mark-up that is placed on most of the goods sold. Former area manager, Paul Price, told *World in Action* that 'He buys the cheapest products to sell in his shops. Embarrassingly so given the number of returned vibrators and marital aids, including things that went rusty when they shouldn't. He buys cheap and sells expensive but he's accumulated a wealth, he's done it himself so you've got to respect him for that. Whether you like him personally is another matter. I've never actually sat down and thought about it but you have to respect his business acumen.'[12]

There are numerous examples of the Private Shops' unusually high mark-ups. Vibrators, advertised in Sullivan magazines for £1.95, retailed in the shops for between £15 and £20. Magazines that cost just a few pence to produce sold for up to £10. But if the mark-ups were outrageous, so were many of the products. Paul Price visited Conegate's warehouse in Stratford, east London, where a number of sex creams were being produced. He watched the manufacturing process with amazement. 'When I was there I saw erection cream and bust development cream being produced on site. It was being made with blackcurrant juice and a bit of yeast. Then they printed the labels and put it into plastic bottles. God knows what effect it had.'

Another way in which the Private Shops maximized profitability was to change the covers of the videos and magazines they sold, making them appear to be more pornographic than was actually the case – a tactic originally pioneered by David Sullivan and Bernard Hardingham when they traded as Subdean Publishing. Paul Price recalls how pornographic Rodox *Color Climax* covers were put on Conegate's own relatively tame videos, thus massively increasing their profit potential. According to Price, 'If you could make something look really hard core you could charge anything up to £200 for it.' Price claims that these scams were always carried out with the company's knowledge and agreement. He says, 'It was part of the deal.'

John East believes that Sullivan's critics have overemphasized these relatively harmless confidence tricks. He points out that the company could not legally sell hard-core pornography and argues that many of its products should not be taken too seriously anyway. 'If you buy erection cream in a sex shop, you're not going to go back in and say you didn't get an erection. There's a very strong connection between the objects he sold in those days and laughter and humour. You look at the product, you look at an enormous vibrator, you look at a girl with an incredible bust. It's not going to harm anybody. It's funny.'

One company that didn't find it funny was Denmark's Rodox Corporation. It was, and probably remains, the producer of the hardest pornography in the world. Its high-quality *Color Climax* magazines and videos deal in graphic detail with everything from lesbian and watersport activities to full animal sex. Rodox claims to be a legitimate international corporation that provides an excellent product for its customers and that only sells in countries with liberal pornography laws. Because of the Obscene Publications Act, Rodox has never attempted to trade in Britain and its products have acquired both a reputation and a rarity value among UK collectors, who will pay a premium for anything bearing the Rodox name. David Sullivan's Conegate company was determined to cash in on this and started producing soft-core imitation Rodox magazines and videos in bulk. Predictably, the Rodox Corporation was determined to stamp this out. Rodox believed that its international reputation would suffer if Sullivan's bogus products were allowed to continue unchallenged, and also that these fakes could prevent Rodox from taking advantage of any subsequent easing of the British pornography laws. Rupert James, Rodox's English-language editor, recalls getting increasingly annoyed at Sullivan's abuse of the name. '*Rodox* is the name of one of our magazines and it is also the name of our parent company so he abused the Rodox name in two ways. He has also copied other of our magazine covers, including our flagship *Color Climax*, *Teenage Sex* and *Blue Climax*.'

Paul Price was one of a number of Conegate employees who saw how Sullivan's imitations were produced and sold. 'The magazines were made to look like continental imported magazines. Anything that was risky was either blanked out, had a star or a spot put over it or was airbrushed over so that you couldn't actually see anything that could be construed as hard-core material. They would use names like *Color Climax* or *Rodox* and you'd look for the best picture in the magazine and try and make it look as though it was something more than it actually was. Obviously the better it looked, the more money you could charge.'[13]

Rodox had first become aware of the Sullivan scam in 1977 but didn't act until 1979. According to Rupert James, Rodox was more concerned about the loss of reputation than any loss of revenue. 'We weren't anxious to get any compensation, we were more anxious to make the world at large aware of the fact we were not connected with him in any way. There were a lot of people who complained, a lot of people who sent letters saying we think your company is behind this. We wanted to make some sort of gesture, to make the world aware we weren't behind this.'

The Rodox Corporation hired Gary Murray, a private detective, to investigate Sullivan's operation. He quickly assembled enough evidence to show beyond reasonable doubt that Conegate was indeed producing its own soft-core version of *Color Climax*. Rodox then hired Edward Cohen, an English barrister, to advise it on how to proceed. Initially it seemed straightforward enough and Cohen, in his written opinion, identified three possible ways forward:

> It seems to me the company has three possible causes of action against Conegate in respect of the publication and sale of Conegate's *Color Climax* magazine, namely:
> 1) Infringement of the company's registered trade mark,
> 2) Passing off, and,
> 3) Breach of copyright.

Cohen advised that the evidence strongly suggested an intention on Conegate's part to deceive its customers. After all, they had adopted the Rodox spelling of *Color*, they had given their magazine the same issue number as the Rodox original and they had even written on their version 'Now legally on sale in Great Britain for the first time.' But Cohen went on to advise that the Rodox Corporation would never win in an English court.

Cohen argued that, paradoxically, any trade-mark action would founder because of the Rodox Corporation's determination to observe the UK law. A trade mark could only be protected if the company intended to use it and, as things stood, that was simply not possible.

Cohen then argued that, while it was undoubtedly Conegate's

intention to 'pass off' their magazine as the Rodox original, it would be difficult to show that customers had been confused. He was not convinced that people would come to court and give evidence that they had sought hard-core pornography and been deceived by Conegate's pale imitation. Furthermore, Cohen doubted that the court would actually back a company that produced hard-core pornography against one that chose not to do so. Cohen felt, on balance, that the court would not intervene to prevent the passing off.

Cohen's final argument, on copyright, followed a similar vein. He said it was unlikely that any court would uphold copyright of obscene material and baldly concluded, at the end of his twenty-page opinion, 'I am of the view that the company will not succeed in any proceedings that may be commenced by it in this country against Conegate to restrain Conegate from using the name *Color Climax* in the field of pornographic material.'

The Rodox Corporation was staggered. Apparently they had no legal redress against Conegate. David Sullivan was going to get away with it. Rupert James was outraged: 'He misleads people. He uses a competitor's reputation for good quality as an advertising aid in order to mislead your average punter into thinking he is buying something of quality whereas in fact he is buying a third-rate copy and not even a total copy either but just the cover and certainly not the contents.'

If Conegate's extraordinary profitability owed much to its willingness to sell poor-quality products, to mark up stock aggressively and to disregard copyrights, it owed as much again to its highly motivated and well-trained employees. Conegate had developed a set of sales techniques that were virtually unique in Britain. Most could be found in the more esoteric training manuals but few companies would have dared to implement them. The methods were not always fair to the customer but they were certainly successful for the company. In some ways, the Private Shops could genuinely claim to be at the cutting edge of retail selling in Britain.

The philosophy that underpinned Conegate's sales strategy is called 'trading up'. It is a particularly ambitious form of retailing. Most sales staff would be content with simply making a sale, but trading up demands much more. It involves persuading the customer that he can get a better deal by making a further purchase at a supposedly discounted price. It was Paul Price's responsibility to teach new staff how to trade up prospective customers. 'You'd show them the techniques, you'd show them the patter and you might even go into the psychology of laying out expensive packs on the magazine racks and flamboyantly saying, "Pick another one out at half price," so they'd spend another forty or fifty pounds. It was extremely high-pressure selling. There have been cases where people have come in to spend ten pounds and gone out after spending three or four hundred pounds. The whole point of teaching the staff was to get them to trade up all the time. If anyone was found not trying to trade up, it was probably a sackable offence.'

Martin Kennard became very successful at this form of selling and regularly traded up clients, sometimes persuading them to spend ten times what they had originally planned. Kennard remembers that Conegate even produced goods and designed a pricing structure solely to make it easier to trade up customers. 'Trading up meant taking the customer to the maximum price you could get from them. If, for argument's sake, they bought something for an odd number like £5.50, you had specific magazines you could trade up with that were priced at £1.50, but you could say, "Well, I'll chuck that in for 50p just to round it up." You could also draw their attention to the marital aids, things like that. Most customers who went into a Private Shop were scared stiff. It was the first time they'd been into a sex shop in their lives. If you were a good salesman you could talk them into buying other products. I mean you could take a customer from £10 to £100. My best take was from a customer that came in for about £15 worth of magazines and we took him to £175.'

Conegate's own internal documentation confirms how fundamental the trading-up strategy was to the company's profitability. Documents sent from head office repeatedly emphasized its importance. For example, one note to area supervisors shows how they could check if shop managers were trading up correctly, simply by examining the daily sales receipts:

This record of sales is vital. It will show you:
a) If a manager is selling stock too cheaply.

b) If he is failing to use a cheap magazine like *Experience* to trade up correctly.

c) If he is achieving a high enough average for each customer. A shop may appear to be doing quite well in terms of weekly turnover – BUT this can be due to a lot of customers coming into the shop *or* the manager selling well to those coming into the shop.

d) If he is selling batteries with each vibrator or creams and lingerie with sex dolls.

With every item that is sold there is always something else that can be sold.

Trading-up techniques were even used when a customer returned to complain about a previous purchase. It often required the sales assistant to show considerable bravery as well as presence of mind. The protesting customer would be taken to one side and the inferior nature of the product would be explained away as being designed only 'for the punters'. Since the complainant had come back he was clearly a 'connoisseur' and therefore much better and harder material would be made available from the back of the store, but 'at a price'. Martin Kennard says it worked almost every time. 'If a customer came back and rucked about the quality of the magazine then you'd pressure sell him even harder. I've had customers that have spent £15 come back screaming and shouting that we'd sold them rubbish. So we've sold them another pack and they've forked out another £15 or £20 and walked away very happy about it.'

It was just as well that Kennard's customer purchased the second magazine pack, since Conegate had a strict rule forbidding refunds. According to Paul Price, 'The company policy was that people didn't get refunds. It was only when the company was actually taken to court, on the rare occasions that a member of the public had the courage to do it, that refunds were given and then the money didn't come out of the till but from head office.'

To ensure that these rules were followed, Conegate instituted a vigorous system of staff testing. The testing of employees is, of course, normal business practice, but Conegate carried it to extremes. For example, area managers such as Price were sent to shops where they were not known to find out if the rules were being followed in all circumstances. 'You had to test the bottle of managers so you were sent in to rap really hard and to threaten physical violence to see whether or not managers had the bottle to refuse a refund.'

This type of testing also gave Conegate the opportunity to check that their staff were being efficient and honest. After all, large sums of cash were coming into the shops on a regular basis and, as Price remembers, the company was very aware of the possibility of theft. 'The company was absolutely paranoid that someone, apart from themselves, might be making money so the area manager would send out a team of people to see how the staff would cope. After some initial difficulties you'd let them trade you up to see how good their sales technique was. Other times you'd go back in complaining about something to see how they'd cope with that. Head office also had a team of testers that would go out and test the area managers and district managers. Everybody was tested. I should think the managing director tested himself half the time. I wouldn't have thought such a high level of discipline would be attached to a test in Boots. They might check politeness or attentiveness but, short of a rabid double-glazing salesman, I can't think of any other company where people are tested to see if they try and take every last penny off a person when they come in.'

If testing was the stick used by Conegate to keep their staff up to the mark, then bonuses were the carrot. Once again, this is normal business practice but, at Conegate, it was carried to an extreme not often seen elsewhere. According to Paul Price, if a shop manager achieved his target figure and got a bonus the goalposts were invariably moved. 'There was a target figure for every shop and if you'd reached it you'd get a bonus which was nice because the basic wages were not particularly great. The only trouble was, after you'd got the bonus a couple of times the target went up and it was a never-ending story. The managers soon became disillusioned which was why there was such a high turnover of staff. They might have been conning the public but the company was conning them.'

Another reason for the high turnover of staff was the continual conflict between Conegate and the police. One of David Sullivan's biggest fears was a repetition of the Subdean fiasco when a big police raid effectively closed down the company for several weeks.

Conegate took elaborate precautions, both in the Private Shops and at their central warehouse, to ensure that it could never happen to them.

The warehouse was located in a nondescript building on Faraday Road, Stratford, east London. Outside, there were no clues to the fact that this was the very heart of the British sex industry, but inside was a very different story. There were literally thousands of magazines, videos, vibrators and other sex aids stored ready for onward transportation to the Private Shops. To confuse the police, the sheer size of the warehouse had been disguised by the building of a false wall which concealed two-thirds of the available space. Access to the hidden part of the warehouse was through an electro-magnetically controlled door big enough for a fork-lift truck. The door switch itself was hidden beneath the fire-alarm button.

The warehouse was also home to a number of other sex businesses. A busy mail-order operation was run from the premises. Video-duplicating machines worked virtually non-stop. Even the creams and potions sold in the Private Shops were produced here. Every morning a transit van full of sexually explicit material was despatched to a different region of Britain. It was met by an area manager who then took the new stock and distributed it to the individual outlets.

In fact, the goods did not normally go directly to the Private Shops but into the area manager's secret 'stash garage': a private garage located in a quiet residential street that had often been hired under a false name. In this way reserve stock could be safely hidden in the vicinity, ready to be moved into the shop if there was a break-in or a police raid. When Paul Price worked for Conegate he had several 'stash garages' under his control: 'When I started I had four which I used to change regularly. I only actually used one but all the others were full in case the police hit more than one shop at a time.'

The Private Shops themselves also had a secret supply of stock hidden on the premises. According to Paul Price, 'They'd keep it underneath the counter usually but sometimes in other places around the shop. There would always be one or two of each magazine, enough to cover the shelves, and a few videos as well so that they could open up as soon as the raid was over and then we'd get there with the boxes from the stash garages and restock properly.'[14]

Police raids held few terrors for the more experienced Private Shop staff but they worried many of the newer employees, as Martin Kennard remembers. 'The first time you were in a police raid was very frightening because you didn't know what was happening. Suddenly you'd have half a dozen police walk in and slap a writ on the table and start seizing everything. At first it's quite frightening but, after a while, we handled so many raids it became a complete and utter joke. As fast as they were taking stuff out of the front we were restocking from the back.' Paul Price recalls a similar incident: 'The police had gone out and forgotten to leave a document. As they came back in there was stuff already on the shelves. But since the warrant was only for one visit, they were unable to remove the stock that had been put back up.'

Conegate did its best to try to protect its staff and minimize the problems. One internal document dealt explicitly with procedures for police raids: 'In the event of a police raid, the managers should give their names and addresses only. They should describe themselves as sales assistants, not managers.' Price explained why this was such a necessary measure: 'If you said you were a manager of a shop or an area manager connected with the business, there's every chance you could be arrested, taken in and questioned. By saying you were a sales assistant they would question you, take a statement in the shop and then leave you to continue trading.'[15]

Ironically Conegate actually tried very hard to prevent hard-core pornography from being sold in its shops. Despite telling customers the exact opposite and prominently displaying signs saying, 'It's porn . . . Porn is all we sell,' it was made very clear to the shop managers that 'Our policy is not to sell illegal material. We sell only material we feel is inside the law. Selling porn under the counter will lead to instant dismissal and prosecution.' Price confirms Conegate's claim: 'The company was adamant that you weren't allowed to sell hard-core pornography because anyone caught selling hard core could be sent to prison including the management of the company. Anyone selling hard core was in fact sacked.'

Conegate's considerable achievements should not be discounted simply because it is in the sex business. In less than four years and in the face of substantial opposition, David Sullivan's Private Shop chain had expanded from just one shop in Soho to more than 100 shops nationwide. Sullivan himself tried to play down Conegate's phenomenal success. He modestly told the *Financial Times*, 'Sex shops are just like any other business. Once you've got enough outlets the economies of scale are enormous. You can cut out the wholesalers and buy the sex aids and stuff direct from the manufacturers in Hong Kong.'[16]

In its 1981 accounts, Conegate reported a massive £2 million profit. In financial terms it was an extraordinary success story. Few new businesses could claim to have done so well so quickly, as Martin Kennard points out: 'I would consider the company at the time to be very well run, very well run indeed. The entire object was profit. Profit was the be-all and end-all of it. It was Thatcherite before Margaret Thatcher. The entire attitude of the company was to make money. It didn't matter what you did, what you told the customer. You created an interest, quoted a price and closed the sale. That was the whole thing. You made money, you pushed it.'

But David Sullivan had actually pushed it too far. Conegate's financial success had been achieved by refusing to compromise or back down under any circumstances, and this had earned him powerful enemies. The new Conservative government might believe in a free market but it also believed in family values. Sullivan and his company were going to be dealt with – one way or another.

NOTES

1. *London Programme*, 5 March 1982.
2. Ibid.
3. Ibid.
4. Ibid.
5. Ibid.
6. Ibid.
7. *World in Action*, 21 September 1992.
8. *News of the World*, February 1982.
9. Ibid.
10. Ibid.

11. Ibid.
12. *World in Action*, 21 September 1992.
13. Ibid.
14. Ibid.
15. Ibid.
16. *Financial Times*, 14 August 1991.

CHAPTER FIVE

JAILBIRD

David Sullivan's decision to move his sex empire into the provinces had completely wrong-footed the authorities. They had not anticipated either the speed or the success of the Private Shops' advance. Local councils found themselves powerless to intervene, as planning permission was not required for sex shops and direct appeals to Conegate's better nature were virtually useless. Part of the reason for this was the siege mentality adopted by Sullivan and his senior managers. The Private Shops had originally encountered tremendous opposition and no one had wanted to sit down and discuss the issues properly. Now, after three years of hard battle and with his enemies routed, Sullivan was in no mood for compromise.

It became clear to the authorities that the only way to control the spread of the Private Shops was to bring in new legislation and, after considerable lobbying, the Conservative government was persuaded to act. They decided to introduce a section into the 1982 Local Government (Miscellaneous Provisions) Bill requiring the licensing of sex shops. Technically, the Bill was targeted at all sex shops, which were now considered to be a growing nuisance by the authorities. David and Ralph Gold had started to follow Sullivan's example by expanding their Ann Summers chain and other sex entrepreneurs were also beginning to jump on the bandwagon. But Conegate was the government's main target and, in particular, its owner David Sullivan.

Patrick Mayhew, then a Home Office minister, outlined the provisions of the Bill on London Weekend Television's *London Programme*: 'What the Bill says is this. If the local authority reckons that the applicant is unsuitable to run a sex shop, whether because he's had a previous conviction or for any other reason, then they can refuse a licence. Equally they can say, "We're going to refuse a licence," if they think, having regard to the locality, it would be inappropriate for the application to be granted. These are the two criteria that the authorities can apply. But they wouldn't be able to say, "No sex shops because we don't like sex shops or because we object to the morality of sex shops." That's outside the provisions of the Bill.'[1]

What Mayhew left unexplained was the strategy that underpinned the legislation. His emphasis on the probity of the licensee had a subtext to it that David Sullivan immediately recognized. In 1979, Sullivan had been charged with the relatively serious offence of living off immoral earnings. It was alleged that he and three others had run two brothels, one at the Park Sauna in Romford Road, Manor Park, and the other at Nicole's Sauna in Kentish Town Road. Sullivan realized that if he was convicted the Private Shops would not be licensed and their very survival could be at stake.

David Sullivan has always believed that the authorities deliberately targeted him as part of a plan to ensure he had a criminal conviction, before introducing licensing laws making it impossible for felons to own sex shops. In fact, this seems unlikely since Sullivan was charged before licensing was really on the political agenda. However, it is possible that the authorities were aware of his impending court case when they considered the licensing provisions and then improvised a plan to ensure that any subsequent conviction would result in the destruction of the Private Shop empire and therefore a significant reduction in the number of provincial sex shops.

For a variety of reasons David Sullivan's case would not finally come to court until April 1982 and so Conegate, aware of the potentially disastrous consequences of a Sullivan conviction, decided to use the time to launch a number of initiatives against licensing. Brian Richards, Conegate's retail director, began a highly successful 'Support your local sex shop' campaign. It involved persuading Private Shop customers to sign petitions, lobby councillors and write to their MPs objecting to licensing. Paul Price claims that the campaign was surprisingly well supported: 'Thousands and thousands put their names down. Very rarely did people refuse to sign when they came into the shop.'

Richards even went as far as placing an advertisement in the *News of the World*. It was headed 'We have the right to survive' and claimed to be 'a personal appeal on behalf of 351 employees, 20,000 ordinary workers who are directly or indirectly reliant on the sex industry for their jobs, and your freedom of choice.' The advert then went on to outline comprehensively the arguments against sex-shop licensing:

> There is a Bill presently going through Parliament known as the Local Government (Miscellaneous Provisions) Bill which is expected to become law soon. It sounds innocent enough but its implications for freedom of choice and the job security of our staff and suppliers is frightening. Simply, within one month of it becoming law, it could lead to the closure of all sex shops throughout the country without compensation and without any right of appeal by the owners or representations by customers of sex shops.
>
> The jobs of the people employed by sex shops and their supply industries will be reliant on the whim of local councils who have no mandate from the electorate to take such action. Equally local councils do not have the right to deny the 700,000 customers who use our shops the freedom to buy what they choose, where they choose, when they choose . . .
>
> The closing of sex shops in this country will not remove the demand for our services as the opposition to the sex-shop industry likes to believe. The demand will remain, so will the supply. Simply the supply of sex products will go underground, operated by unscrupulous people who, at best, will pay neither tax or VAT. Our contribution to the government coffers in tax and VAT will be £2 million this year. Revenue they will not be able to collect in the future.
>
> There can be little doubt that the majority of people have no objection to our shops. Our opponents argue that sex shops encourage sexual violence yet last year, during which we doubled our number of outlets by adding nearly sixty branches to our chain, sex crimes dropped by 2,000 and rape came down 13 per cent.

The advertisement concluded by inviting supporters to write to the Home Secretary, Willie Whitelaw. The fact that Conegate was prepared to purchase such a large advert and run such a high-profile campaign showed just how worried it had become about sex-shop licensing, as Paul Price remembers. 'They took it very seriously. We had to cut out all the clippings in the local paper, make notes on all the people opposed to the shops, attend meetings and record conversations at the meetings, anything like that they took very seriously. Any manager who didn't follow the rules or guidelines was out of a job very quickly.'

David Sullivan's brother Clive, still using the name Frank, tried a different approach. He spent months lobbying parliament, arguing that the Miscellaneous Provisions Bill should be watered down because its proposals were either impractical or unnecessary. He went on the record saying, 'We do not really believe there is any need for licences in the first place but, as the government seems intent on introducing some form of licensing scheme, we accept the practicalities of politics and our main concern at the moment is to ensure that the Bill becomes a workable Act.'[2] Eventually his efforts met with some limited success and the final Act did not force councils to license sex shops but instead allowed them to choose whether or not to adopt its voluntary provisions. To this day, some councils still do not require sex shops to be licensed.

The third strand of the new Conegate offensive involved setting up as many new sex shops as possible. David Sullivan realized that, even if he was found not guilty, he could still lose a large number of Private Shops simply by local councils adopting the Act and then deciding that the shops were out of character with the area. Price recalls the mad buying spree that Conegate went on immediately preceding the introduction of licensing: 'They had a target of eighty-five/ninety shops but they went for as many as they could get, realizing that they were going to lose a lot of licensing applications. I don't think they ever believed that the shops would be shut down everywhere. I think what they had in mind was to have more shops than they needed so they could shrink back to a set number. They could then afford to lose a few to make it look like they were losing the fight in some quarters.' Conegate pushed on steadily from 100 Private Shops to a peak total of 128. This meant that, even in a worst-case scenario, a sufficient number would survive to ensure the continuation of the business. It also meant that Conegate had become the biggest sex-shop chain in the world.

Another element of the campaign against licensing involved a concerted attempt by Conegate to change its image. David Sullivan decided to hire several influential people unconnected with the sex industry in an attempt to persuade councils that Conegate was really a respectable organization. He contacted a PR company and also placed an advert in *The Times* asking for a 'liberal-minded' administrator with a background in either the police or the forces to join his company. Better still, 'a member of the nobility'.

Sullivan was in luck. Earl Grey, whose family had given their name to the scented tea, was approached and agreed to take the job for a salary of approximately £15,000 per annum. He was already involved in the sex-shop debate, having spoken against the Local Government (Miscellaneous Provisions) Bill in the House of Lords on the grounds that it restricted personal freedom and intruded on civil liberties. Grey was not introduced to David Sullivan, whose trial was imminent, but to his brother, Clive Sullivan. Grey was told that they shared the same liberal political outlook and that with him as a non-executive director Conegate would be able more effectively to challenge old and reactionary councils.

The second non-executive director recruited by Conegate was Major Peter James. He had previously served with the Royal Worcestershire Regiment before joining the prison service. James told the *News of the World*, 'If anyone thinks I'm a bit odd taking up an appointment with a chain of sex shops they're entitled to say that. But someone has to make sure the shops are properly run otherwise they can go underground and fall into the wrong hands. Since I was offered the appointment I have had a look at one and I wasn't shocked or surprised.' David Sullivan added that 'The Major feels it's important to demonstrate publicly that support for the availability of adult material isn't limited to sex-shop customers but extends to an even greater range of the population.'[3]

Paul Price believes that these two unusual appointments helped Conegate in its licensing battles. 'I think it made the letter headings look proper and they were potentially useful weapons at council meetings. They were public figures. Their names gave weight to the company. They could be bandied about to show that it was an upright and moral company, a proper company, as opposed to belonging to someone who had been busted for living off immoral earnings.'

With Earl Grey and Major Peter James now on board, Conegate started to contest sex-shop licences aggressively. Martin Kennard even remembers the two new non-executive directors turning up at one licence hearing in a blue Rolls-Royce. 'Conegate brought out every person they could get to make it look legitimate and supposedly some very influential people were brought in. You fought tooth and nail to get the shop licensed by the council. There was a lot of money to be made. I mean, when you received a licence to run a shop, basically it was a licence to print money.'

If hiring respectability was less than subtle, the final part of Conegate's licensing initiative was positively outrageous. It involved pointing out the company's possible response to any failure to obtain a licence. The new legislation meant local councils might be able to stop sex shops in their areas, but there were things worse than sex shops, as Clive Sullivan grimly reminded them on the *London Programme*: 'A sex shop that doesn't get a licence is a building that represents a substantial investment and the company would look for a return on that investment. One of the alternatives it could possibly consider would be nude encounter parlours.'[4] Nude encounter parlours, which were not covered by the licensing provisions of the Act, were briefly popular in Soho. They were places where men could spend time and money talking to naked women about their sexual problems. The women would also try to sell them merchandise to complement the 'therapy'. These nude encounter parlours were just one of a number of ideas put forward by the sex-industry bosses to intimidate provincial councillors into leaving the sex shops alone.

There were other loopholes in the legislation as well. One, which Conegate later exploited, revolved around the definition of a sex shop. A sex shop is legally defined as a shop which primarily stocks sex products. If it stocks a majority of other products it is not a sex shop and therefore does not require a licence. Clive Sullivan saw an opportunity here as well: 'If you have a sex shop as a sex shop fully, then it needs a licence. But if you have a large department store that sublets part of their store, then you will have a sex shop within a department store which would not require a licence because it does not represent a substantial proportion of the turnover of the store as a whole.'[5]

This mixture of lateral thinking, lobbying and intimidation served Conegate well and the initial licensing round was not as destructive as the company had originally feared. Many of the councils that adopted the provisions decided to accept the *status quo*, keep the existing Private Shops and reject all future applicants. The few councils that did decide to reject Conegate's applications found their decisions repeatedly challenged and even subject to judicial review.

If David Sullivan felt pleasure at the success of Conegate's tactics, it was probably diminished by the knowledge that his own court case, with its possible consequences for the Private Shops, could not be delayed much longer. The road to Snaresbrook Crown Court had been anything but straightforward but now the journey was almost over.

The reason for the two-year delay was an improper approach made to Sullivan soon after his arrest. He was told that a payment of £45,000 would ensure the case was dropped. Sullivan hired a private detective to investigate the offer and then reported it to Scotland Yard's anti-corruption squad. They arrested four men, including Joseph Ross of Grosvenor Gardens, Pimlico, and Gary Reynolds of New Quebec Street, Marylebone. All four pleaded not guilty to the charges and it was decided that this case needed to be resolved before Sullivan's own trial could commence. The case came before the Old Bailey in February 1981.

The prosecution alleged that the men had all conspired to persuade Sullivan that they were senior police officers and could help him by giving perjured evidence in exchange for money. Sullivan told the court, 'I just thought what was going on was wrong. I thought something should be done.' In fact, Sullivan later came to regret his public-spiritedness. The tabloid press used the trial as a pretext to examine his colourful life, which Sullivan feared would adversely affect his own impending court case. He remarked at the time, 'All I've had is aggravation. This case has caused me a lot of problems. There is no benefit to me. I wonder why I bothered. Newspapers have called me a vice boss. This is very detrimental to me going to court on a vice charge. I have no previous convictions.'[6] This, of course, was untrue, though his past offences had not been as serious as those he now faced. Eventually both Ross and Reynolds were convicted of conspiracy to defraud David Sullivan; the other two were acquitted, one after a retrial. Now that this was out of the way Sullivan could finally enter the dock himself.

Sullivan was accused of living off immoral earnings in two ways: by directly receiving a percentage of prostitutes' income and by advertising their services in his magazines. Predictably, the case attracted substantial media attention, increased by the realization that Sullivan, still only thirty-three, had just become Britain's highest-paid executive, having earned £325,000 in the previous twelve months and received a further £418,000 in pension contributions from his master company, Roldvale. He was charged along with three others: Cecil Jackson, who was said to have delivered the takings to Sullivan; Stephen Foster, who was said to have run Nicole's Sauna; and his wife, Bridget Foster, who was said to have run the Park Sauna.

Mr Paul Purnell, prosecuting, outlined the case by saying, 'Sullivan received a cut from the takings and through his magazines which advertised them in terms directed precisely to the prostitution element.' Purnell went on to explain that in the saunas 'all sorts of lewd sexual activities by women took place for money'. The girls stripped off and their clients were offered 'special extras'. These girls were relatively poorly paid and were exploited by Sullivan. One of them, called Sally, had told the police that she earned all her money by providing sexual favours.

The police had kept watch on the saunas for several months. Sergeant Michael Hoskins said that when he went in for a massage a young masseuse asked him if he wanted extra services, but he declined. The police had visited the Park Sauna a total of sixteen times and, on each occasion, had been made aware of the extra services on offer. A price list was found by the police when they raided the sauna showing that costs varied from £5 for a straight sauna to £9 for an assisted bath and £20 for a massage performed by a naked girl. Sergeant Hoskins then told the court that he had once followed Cecil Jackson from the Park Sauna to Sullivan's office in nearby Upton Lane. When Jackson was arrested he had £401 in his pocket and a further £1,831 in his briefcase. Jackson told the police it was his money and had nothing to do with David Sullivan.

Sullivan himself admitted visiting both saunas using the assumed name of Don Bell. He said, 'I didn't want to be recognized because I wanted to be treated the same as other customers.' He told the court, 'I had no direct interest in the saunas. I only visited them as a customer and was never offered sexual services ... I promoted them in my magazines because I thought they were friendly, clean places. I never thought from the contents of those magazines that it would be possible to be prosecuted.'

The jury found Sullivan and his three other defendants all guilty as charged. Judge Ian McLean jailed Sullivan for nine months and ordered him to pay £10,000 costs, saying, 'It is clear that you were, through your very forceful personality, the driving force behind Jackson and, through him, the brothels.' Judge McLean then described Jackson as 'Sullivan's lackey' and imprisoned him for four months with £500 costs. Finally, he jailed both Stephen and Bridget Foster for two months with £500 costs each.

The tabloid press pounced on David Sullivan's conviction. On 16 May 1982 the *News of the World* ran a full-page splash headlined 'King porn is caged at last' and subtitled 'It looks like curtains for David Sullivan's sex shop empire'. Certainly it was difficult to see what Sullivan could do next. The newspaper even quoted a resigned-sounding Clive Sullivan admitting, 'We may have to sell up. But who will pay the proper value when the licences are in doubt?'[7]

One possible solution considered by David Sullivan was to try to float Conegate on the stock market. This had been in his mind for some time and it may have even figured in his decision to recruit Earl Grey and Major James. He outlined his scheme to the *Daily Mail*'s Patrick Sergeant just before the trial:

Last year we made £2.8 million. This year we'll reach between £3 million and £3.5 million. I'm only asking £10 million because of the nature of the business.

I've got 120 Private Shops spread over the country and I own the freehold on 100 of them. At cost alone they represent nearly £3 million in the £4.5 million of assets shown on the balance sheet. Sex will be the growth industry of the eighties, just like betting shops were in the sixties and casinos in the seventies. Ours is a perfectly normal business run by ordinary, nice people

– not gangsters. We do lose stock from police raids but it's not a major problem. We build it into our costs and so the public end up paying more than they should. Our profit margins are high.

I'd love to come to the stock market. We've got a track record, a management structure and a far better future than many companies which are quoted. What's more, I can assure you that we shall meet our profits forecast.[8]

The problem was, as Patrick Sergeant reported, that no merchant bank was prepared to sponsor the launch. In those circumstances a Conegate flotation was not really a possibility. Nor was an outright purchase, despite Sullivan's attempts to talk up interest. He told Sergeant, 'I nearly sold out to a public company last year. But they wanted us on the cheap with warranted profits and time to pay. They'd have bought it with my money.'[9] However, no company was ever named and it seems unlikely that a sale to a public company was ever a real possibility. Sullivan, now serving time in Ford Open Prison, was both figuratively and literally stuck.

While Sullivan pondered the future, Brian Richards, Conegate's retail director, did his best to keep up staff morale. He wrote a special message to all employees responding to the unflattering media attention. After commenting that the 'media propaganda', as he called it, against Conegate was simply aimed at selling more newspapers, he went on with a flourish:

Let me assure you that your jobs are secure and that I have no intention of losing or closing any shops as long as they are making profit. Our only concern at the moment is the licensing Bill and this will not be affected by the recent publicity we have received, but we still need to fight with our petitions etc.

Please remember that Conegate have more shops than Woolworths; we have the sales staff, the premises and the distribution to sell any commodity we choose, and what difference does it make whether we sell sex or hamburgers? You are the sales staff, you work for Conegate, you do have a secure job and a secure future.

Despite Richards's comforting letter, the Private Shop employees knew they were in deep trouble. Martin Kennard remembers the period well. 'The Miscellaneous Provisions Bill stipulated, purely and simply, that anybody with a criminal record was not suitable to run or hold a licence for a sex shop and the result of David's court case was common knowledge. It was a tense period for everybody.'

In the meantime, David Sullivan had taken his case to the Court of Appeal and was finally released after serving seventy-one days in prison. Cecil Jackson also had his sentence reduced. Lord Justice O'Connor, the appeal court judge, said the lower court had been right to impose jail terms but that three months each would have sufficed. The girls had not been corrupted or forced into prostitution by the two men, Sullivan's previous convictions were not serious and Jackson had previously been of good character.

Sullivan's enforced period of inactivity had given him plenty of time to reflect on his life and many people claim that he came out of prison a changed man. John East says that he saw a noticeable difference. 'I think it caused him to think about his future and how he could make money and I think he realized his former business was a dangerous one to be in and it would be easier without the sex shops. Up to that time he had made fun of everybody. Now Big Brother had come and clapped him inside and so he thought. "Right, I'll come out and I will get round this come hell or high water." '[10]

By the end of the summer Sullivan had indeed worked out how to get round it. He suddenly announced that he had sold his sex businesses to Brian Richards. Despite Sullivan's earlier disparaging comments about one company's attempt to buy Conegate 'with my money', the sale was apparently to be funded through an earn-out.

David Sullivan seized every opportunity to tell the world that he was out of the sex business for good. He went on London Weekend Television's *After Midnight* programme and said, 'I don't run a porn empire any more. I retired. I'm talking as a person who used to be in the business.'[11] He even included the claim in advertisements for the newspapers he went on to found, saying, 'My name is David Sullivan. I used to publish girlie magazines and owned Britain's biggest chain of sex shops. Now I publish *Sunday Sport*.'[12]

Brian Richards also wasted no time in telling people of the change of ownership. He wrote a very thorough letter to the Private Shop staff explaining the transfer in some detail:

At the start of 1982 the Private Shops and ancillary operations were owned and run by Conegate Ltd. and in Scotland by its subsidiary, Centrewall Ltd. Conegate Ltd. was a wholly owned subsidiary of Roldvale Ltd., which was a company owned by David Sullivan. While the day-to-day management of Conegate was of no concern to Mr Sullivan, he was the ultimate beneficiary.

During the course of 1982 the Local Government (Miscellaneous Provisions) Act was passed which provided for the licensing of sex shops. In addition, in May 1982, despite the evidence, Mr Sullivan was convicted of living off immoral earnings. The effect of this was firstly that the likelihood of Conegate obtaining licences was considerably reduced and secondly that Mr Sullivan resolved to be no longer in a position where he was a target for false accusations.

Brian Richards's letter then went on to say that he had therefore decided to buy the entire business from David Sullivan and that he now planned to transfer everything including all the Private Shops to a new company called Quietlynn. Earl Grey and Major James had agreed to join the new company's board. All the Private Shop staff would be re-employed on the same terms and conditions as before. Finally, the letter dealt with the subject of David Sullivan and his relationship with Quietlynn, but in a curiously legalistic way:

Mr David Sullivan no longer has any interest in the control or operation of our business, and whilst it is highly unlikely he would seek to do so, employees should be aware that he has no authority over my company's activities or employees.

This claim is at the very heart of the David Sullivan story. He remains proud of his career as a sex baron but says he abandoned it all in 1982 with the sale of the Private Shops and his other sex businesses. For him, prison was a watershed. He admits still to retaining an interest in a couple of 'girlie' magazines but argues these are merely remnants of his past and, anyway, they belong at the tame end of the market. He no longer seeks to challenge the boundaries of acceptability. The new David Sullivan is apparently a very different person. He is a successful newspaper proprietor looking to expand into other legitimate media-related activities. He simply wants a little respect and a quiet life.

It was this claim that was examined most closely by the *World in Action* programme transmitted in September 1992. The production team wanted to know if David Sullivan had really left the porn business ten years earlier, as he said. Should he be treated as a legitimate newspaper proprietor? Or was he still pulling the strings of the biggest sex empire Britain has ever seen? The programme spent months talking to people, obtaining documents and studying the evidence. It uncovered link after link between Sullivan and the businesses he claimed to have left behind. The programme eventually concluded that Sullivan remains a pivotal figure in the sex industry to this day.

World in Action discovered that few Private Shop staff ever really believed that Sullivan had relinquished control of the sex shops. There were a number of reasons for their scepticism. The first concerned Brian Richards's ability to raise enough money to purchase the business, even bearing in mind that it was meant to have been mostly an earn-out. Paul Price was one senior manager who found it all very difficult to swallow: 'It was a standing joke in the company as to how Brian had supposedly managed to find all this money. He simply wouldn't have been able to come up with the sort of money that would have needed to have been exchanged for the shops. There was never a figure quoted but, bearing in mind the turnover of the shops and the mail-order side, it had to be a fair number of millions and for an east-London boy like Brian, that was an awful lot of money.'

The second reason for finding Sullivan's claim unconvincing was his continuing presence on the periphery of the business. Price ran into him several times when he visited the headquarters building in Deanery Street, east London. 'On a number of occasions I had to go up to the office to talk with Christine King or Clive Sullivan and, on two occasions, I saw David coming out of Clive's office and the way he came out suggested it wasn't a visit for tea but a business meeting. He walked round as if he owned the place.'

For most staff, the main reason for doubting Sullivan's claim was financial. Martin Kennard was one of a number who found it difficult to believe that someone like Sullivan would walk away from such a profitable venture. 'He was not in a position to be directly in control of the shops purely and simply because he had a criminal record. You're talking about a hell of a lot of money. When I became supervisor of ten shops we had a turnover of £700,000. You don't walk away from money like that. I'm damn sure I wouldn't.'

It wasn't only the Private Shop staff who refused to believe that Sullivan had genuinely sold the business. One former Quietlynn director told *World in Action* that one reason why he resigned was because he came to believe that David Sullivan was still secretly controlling the empire. However, while staff suspicion may be a useful guide, it is not conclusive proof of Sullivan's continuing involvement in his old sex-shop business. *World in Action*'s second revelation was much more damning.

The programme decided to find out who now owns the Private Shops and commissioned over 100 Land Registry searches. The results were startling. Brian Richards and his successors still do not actually own any of the shop freeholds. The properties are all still registered to either Conegate or Roldvale, David Sullivan's two main companies. David Sullivan has always said that he cut all his links with the Private Shops in 1982 and this discovery clearly undermines that claim. But his position is just about tenable provided these are simply passive investments purchased and let to the Private Shops before 1982. However, his credibility would be damaged substantially by the acquisition of additional Private Shop premises after 1982, which would suggest a degree of cooperation between himself and his old business that he has always vigorously denied.

World in Action identified no less than three Private Shop properties acquired by Conegate since 1982, and there may be more since the Land Registry was unable to complete all the searches with the information available. The first was in Cardiff Road, Newport, and was registered in May 1989; the second was in Moorfields, Liverpool, registered in February 1990 and the third was in Bootham, York, registered in March 1990. This meant that Conegate was still identifying and purchasing Private Shop properties years after Sullivan claimed to have severed all connections with the sex industry.

The Private Shop employees appear to have been right all along: a close relationship still remains between Sullivan and the Private Shop bosses.

The third link uncovered by *World in Action* effectively shattered Sullivan's increasingly unconvincing claims to be out of the sex industry. The Private Shops have a promotional tour every year during which a top glamour girl spends a day in each shop meeting the clients. Tara Bardot, the editor of David Sullivan's *Titbits* magazine and a regular *Daily Sport* model, has taken part in several of these tours. She unwittingly revealed that her tours were funded not by the Private Shop organization but by Roldvale, David Sullivan's master company. While there may be some minor benefit to David Sullivan's publications, the primary purpose of the tours is to publicize the Private Shops. Sullivan's financing of them leads inevitably to the conclusion that he must still have an interest in promoting the sex shops. Former *Sunday Sport* editor Ian Pollack is in no doubt as to who really benefits. He received a memo from David Sullivan in June 1992 instructing him to feature Tara as their 'big Page Three, listing all her dates and giving the dates a decent amount of space'. This was not a paid advert and, according to Pollack, 'it could only have helped the shops'.

None the less, and despite all of *World in Action*'s suspicions, up to now it has been impossible to say categorically that Sullivan remains the beneficial owner of the sex businesses he claims to have left behind. The new evidence that follows takes the matter beyond any reasonable doubt.

Many observers of the sex industry have commented on the fact that Sport Newspapers carry far more Private Shop advertising than any other newspaper group, despite its smaller circulation. But what has not been known is the extraordinary degree of David Sullivan's knowledge about the response rates to the adverts. John Bull, another former editor of the *Sunday Sport*, remembers receiving a number of complaints from readers who had tried to use the Private Shop mail-order service: 'I rang David and said, "Can you do something about this? there were twelve complaints today." There was a pause and he said, "Do you know how many items were sold last week out of that warehouse?" I said, "No" and he said, "47,000."

I said, "OK David, I'll shut up." Twelve complaints out of 47,000, forget it.'

Ian Pollack also noticed the extremely close relationship between David Sullivan and the Private Shops. 'Whenever we wanted to get sex aids or blow-up dolls to go with a feature we would just go down to the local Private Shop, say where we were from, and take the goods away. We didn't normally return them and, as far as I remember, we were never invoiced for them. I always understood they were David's shops. He always referred to them as "my shops".'

Other Sport Newspapers editors tell similar stories. At least four have said that David Sullivan referred to the Private Shops as 'my shops' and one went so far as to claim that Sullivan had become depressed because his shops were doing so badly. Even David Sullivan's friends occasionally let the cat out of the bag. In one unguarded moment John East said, 'Look at the *Sunday Sport*, it's teeming with his own advertisements.'

But the piece of evidence that does most to damage David Sullivan's claim to have quit the sex industry is a memo he sent to Ian Pollack expressing concern at the amount of free publicity some sex magazines were getting in Sport Newspapers. Sullivan wrote, 'We often seem to run plugs in the paper for sets in *Penthouse* and other girlie mags. There is a feeling that we should "self promote" our girlie titles more, in particular *Playbirds*, *Rustler* and *Whitehouse*.' Two of these magazines were, of course, set up by Sullivan in the 1970s and were among those allegedly sold in 1982. The fact that he still regarded them in 1992 as in-house titles clearly conflicts with earlier claims.

David Sullivan's decision to mislead people over the ownership of both the magazines and the sex shops makes good sense to Paul Price: 'I think that if he had stayed on and had been refused licences then they could have quite legitimately shut him down. This way he maintained the honey pot where he gets his money to open all his newspapers and there's nothing they can do about it.'

The hastily arranged transfer of the Private Shops from Conegate to Quietlynn did not take long to start coming apart at the seams. Within twelve months, Brian Richards, Quietlynn's managing director, had been charged under Section Two of the Obscene

Publications Act and the licences were again in jeopardy. This time the Private Shops' senior management were ready and a complex plan, designed to ensure the long-term survival of the business, was put into operation. It involved a complex restructuring of the group and the setting up of several new companies.

Ray Darker, the northern area manager, formed Sheptonhurst Ltd. (which he later renamed Darker Enterprises). According to a former colleague this was intended to be a 'cleaner than clean' company. All Private Shops that had received a licence were transferred into Sheptonhurst so any conviction suffered by Richards could not rebound on the business.

The second new company formed was called Pabciec (Private Alternative Birth Control Information and Education Centres Ltd.). It provided a home for shops that had failed to get a licence. It originally planned to exploit the gap in the legislation identified by Clive Sullivan whereby some sex products could be sold in a shop if the majority of the stock was not sexual in nature. Pabciec was not a success and was wound up within a couple of years.

Quietlynn itself managed to survive in a much-modified form. Brian Richards was eventually found not guilty but the changes to the company structure had already been made. Quietlynn was only left with shops that were located in areas where licensing was not required.

The most important part of the whole restructuring plan was the creation of a third new company called Limetime Services. This was technically an administration company set up by Christine King and Clive Sullivan, David Sullivan's two most trusted lieutenants. In reality it was to be the new command vehicle for the whole sex-shop empire.

There were two problems in continually juggling shops and companies to maximize licensing opportunities: the enormous administrative headaches caused by the changes and the difficulties in ensuring control remained in the right hands. Christine King's Limetime Services provided an ingenious way round both. Almost everyone in the Private Shop empire above the rank of shop manager was hired by Limetime Services as a senior administrator. Quietlynn, Sheptonhurst and Pabciec then simply contracted Limetime to provide all their management services. Now, if there was

David Sullivan with glamour model Zeta Ross, during a *Daily Star* party at Stringfellows. Sullivan controlled the *Daily Star* for eight turbulent weeks during August and September 1987. (*Rex Features*)

David Sullivan outside Snaresbrook Crown Court in 1982. He was convicted of living off immoral earnings and served 71 days in prison. (*Press Association*)

David Sullivan in his old house at Stradbrook Drive in Chigwell. The distinctive zebra-skin furnishings became his trademark. (*George Richardson/ People in Pictures*)

Sullivan at work. He never goes near Sport Newspapers' offices but continually inundates his editors with faxes and phone calls. (*George Richardson/People in Pictures*)

David Sullivan and Karren Brady just after Roldvale's takeover of
Birmingham City football club. Their later attempt to intimidate the local
newspaper into sponsoring a new stand severely damaged their credibility.
(*News Team International*)

PREVIOUS PAGE: Mary Millington, Britain's first porn queen. Her publicity
stunts included posing topless outside the Houses of Parliament and
10 Downing Street. (*Rex Features*)

Julie Lee, star of 'Emmanuelle in Soho'. She later died in a car crash.
(*Rex Features*)

David Sullivan about to attend the annual general meeting of Bristol Evening Post PLC. Both his proposed motions were defeated. (*News Team International*)

David Sullivan at his new office in Birch Hall. Note the horse-racing memorabilia. Sullivan always works from home. (*Independent*)

revealing. But a more important piece of evidence was the contact address given confidentially by Roldvale to Vodata. That address was 182 Cranbrook Road, Ilford – the home of Limetime Services, the company that controls it all.

NOTES

1. *London Programme*, 5 March 1982.
2. Ibid.
3. *News of the World*, 14 March 1982.
4. *London Programme*, 5 March 1982.
5. Ibid.
6. Press Association, 5 February 1981.
7. *News of the World*, 16 May 1982.
8. *Daily Mail*, 20 January 1982.
9. Ibid.
10. *World in Action*, 21 September 1992.
11. *After Midnight*, 8 December 1983.
12. *Park Lane*, No.18, 1988.

TOP: Birch Hall, Theydon Bois. David Sullivan's achievements are now literally set in marble and stone. (*Chas Clarke/ People in Pictures*)

ABOVE LEFT: Relaxing in his living room. Sullivan is wearing a Birmingham City FC shirt. (*News Team International*)

BELOW LEFT: David Sullivan's magnificent indoor swimming pool. His basement also contains a two-lane bowling alley and a Stringfellows-style dance floor. (*News Team International*)

David Sullivan with his new Bentley. He claims that he has only recently started buying 'really flash' cars. (*News Team International*)

David Sullivan. The Sultan of Sleaze. (*News Team International*)

any juggling to be done, it would not affect the senior m
and Limetime always knew exactly what was going
various businesses.

The system was further refined when Limetime decided
a central banking system. Monies from all three compa
now paid into this one account. Limetime had the mo
brains and almost complete control, as Paul Price re
'Limetime Services is a management company that was s
run the various companies that came after Conegate. I
controls it all. It's where the money goes, it's where the d
are made, it's where the management people are hired and fi

Limetime is now located at 182 Cranbrook Road, Ilford
the Cranbrook pub. Despite its modest surroundings a
profile, it remains the most important company involved
Private Shops. Whoever controls Limetime Services almost d
controls the world's largest sex-shop empire.

One final link has emerged between David Sullivan a
empire he claims to have left behind. Sullivan has said
nothing to do with Limetime Services but, in fact, on
businesses has been secretly using it. That business is Scan C
telephone-sex operation.

Until recently, adult phone lines worked like this. T
themselves, which could cost up to 48 pence per minut
were provided by three companies: British Telecom, Me
Vodata. These were then leased on a wholesale basis to
Providers'. The Service Providers in turn hired out indiv
retail to 'Information Providers'. The Information Provide
organized the telephone recordings and advertised th
Finally, the money was collected by the Service Provide
with the other parties.

David Sullivan was uncharacteristically slow in g
telephone-sex lines and initially only became an Inforr
vider. However, he quickly realized that the real mone
made further up the chain and his master compan
approached Vodata to become a Service Provider. R
the name Scan Calls to conceal its true identity.

The address given by Scan Calls in all its advertisem
Forest Road, Walthamstow, an old Sullivan address a

CHAPTER SIX

SEX ON SUNDAY

David Sullivan always wanted to be a newspaper publisher. His first handwritten attempt was made with his brother, Clive, while they were still at Cogan Primary School in Cardiff. Twenty years later he tried again, this time with the *Private National News*, a US-style scandal sheet. In the early eighties, he held a number of discussions with the print unions about the possibility of launching a London-based sports newspaper. None of these attempts came to anything, but from them all evolved the *Sunday Sport*, David Sullivan's most outrageous creation.

There were a number of motives behind Sullivan's determination to own a national newspaper. Austin Mitchelson, the first editor of the *Sunday Sport*, believes that the most important was an increasing desire for respectability. He remembers Sullivan telling him how he was fed up with being excluded. 'He said that he wanted to be accepted, that he's always been an outsider – a punter – and never part of the establishment. When we were getting into the final preparations for *Sunday Sport* he was coming up with jokes like "We'll get our knighthoods for this," but I think he meant it. Somewhere down the line he would like to be accepted and become Sir David, and why not?'

Sullivan also realized that ownership of a newspaper brought with it a certain amount of power and influence. While the *Sunday Sport* may not itself be the most prestigious of papers, Sullivan's newspaper group as a whole cannot be ignored. Its weekly readership is now measured in millions.

However, those who know David Sullivan best believe there was a far more pragmatic reason behind his decision to launch a national newspaper. According to them it has nothing to do with respectability, power or even influence. John East talked to Sullivan at length before the launch of the *Sunday Sport* about the economic rationale that underpinned it. Sullivan told him that the newspaper was not only a logical and safe alternative to adult magazines but that it also provided a way in which he could advertise his sex products for next to nothing. 'He said, "I'm going to fulfil my great ambition and go into the newspaper business." He had the idea of a glamour newspaper rather than a glamour magazine. The *Sunday Sport* was never taken seriously as a newspaper, it was just an escapist journal, but it was a brilliant ploy. It was cheap and there were a hell of a lot of pages and each page was selling his mail-order business. I dare say the *Sunday Sport* would be profitable if you gave it away as a freesheet.'

Sullivan's market research had shown that nine million adults did not read a Sunday newspaper of any sort. This suggested a gap in the market beneath the existing Sunday tabloids which Sullivan was determined to exploit. He placed an advertisement in one of the newspaper trade journals for an editor. It was seen by Austin Mitchelson, a journalist who had worked in both newspapers and radio.

'It was a fairly vague advert but I wrote a letter and met David Sullivan and we talked about launching a successful bottom-of-the-market tabloid newspaper. David told me he had originally wanted to start a sports newspaper in London but he realized it wasn't going to work so he broadened the concept to make it more like the *People*. Good sport with some other elements in it – nipples, basically. It was going to be a newspaper that made you laugh. It was to be fun. It was a bridge between the comics and newspapers. It was always going to include things that other papers weren't covering. The most famous example was the bomber found on the moon. Stories which were silly, that were just fancied up. You know, you'd go to work and say, "See that in the paper, just fancy that." It was never going to sell five million like the *News of the World* but it should get a good slice of the market. We planned to break even at around 200,000 to 250,000 copies.'

The idea was simple enough and Sullivan could take some comfort from the old adage that no one had ever gone bust under-estimating the market. But in reality setting up a newspaper was a huge financial gamble, as Eddy Shah, who was preparing to launch *Today* at the same time, was just beginning to find out. David Sullivan formed a new company to control the *Sunday Sport*. It was called Apollo Ltd. and was registered on 28 February 1986 with himself and Austin Mitchelson as directors. Later the name would be changed to Sport Newspapers. Mitchelson remembers that the first subject Sullivan wanted to discuss was money. 'He said, "I've got a couple of million pounds lying around to deal with it," and we started off with that as a budget. Providing we didn't spend more than a couple of million everything was going to be fine. So we drew up a large television advertising campaign which was going to swamp the screens for the first week or so and that was going to cost the bulk of the budget. The rest of it was going to go on reporters' salaries and all the other bits and pieces of running a newspaper.'

Then Sullivan dropped two bombshells in quick succession. He told his new editor to prepare for 'a September launch' despite the fact that this was only a few months away and Apollo, as yet, had no offices, no equipment and no staff. He then made it clear that everything was going to be paid for in cash. 'I met him at his office and he said, "You'll need some money to deal with printers, to find offices, put in telephones and things like that." He then reached into his desk and I thought he was going to pull out a cheque book and say, "I've started an account." What in fact happened was that he reached into his desk and brought out several bundles of ten-pound notes. There was about a thousand pounds on that occasion and this continued, the bundles of tenners. I used to have to carry them in a briefcase because they wouldn't fit in my pocket. I always felt there was a huge wad of notes somewhere.'[1]

Mitchelson soon discovered that using cash was just part of a wider plan by Sullivan to keep costs to an absolute minimum. The entire paper was to be produced with less than a dozen full-time journalists. There was to be no high-tech newsroom. Every penny was to be counted. Mitchelson marvelled at the differences between Sullivan's shoe-string approach to *Sunday Sport* and Eddy Shah's state-of-the-art *Today* newspaper:

'I guess Eddy Shah managed to have the computer companies call on him, wire it up and show him how it worked. I drove down to the local Dixons with bundles of tenners and bought as many Amstrad word processors as they could supply, put them in the back of the car and drove back to the office. It was certainly a different sort of financing but that's not to say it didn't work. It was also a natural governor on spending because you could only carry so much money around with you.'

Despite the restrictions placed on Mitchelson, Sullivan became increasingly concerned at the financial risks involved in launching the *Sunday Sport*. Unlike Shah, who was sharing the risk with others, Sullivan was using all his own money. Mitchelson vividly remembers the moment when Sullivan's nerve finally broke. 'He suddenly realized the print run was going to cost him £30,000 a week, he realized that ten journalists cost so much a month and so on. He looked at all this money going out and I think that a little cold sweat came over him and he got cold feet. He still thought it was going to work but why not spread the risk a little and give some to his friends?'

David Sullivan turned for help to David and Ralph Gold, businessmen he had known all his working life. The Golds were still heavily identified with the sex industry. They ran the Ann Summers sex shops and party-plan business from their offices at Whyteleafe in Surrey. They also ran Gold Star Publications, one of the main suppliers of soft-core pornography in Britain. But it was their Moore Harness business that most interested Sullivan. Moore Harness is a major magazine distribution company and the *Sunday Sport* would need all the help it could get if it was going to reach the best retail outlets.

Asking David and Ralph Gold for help may have seemed a little strange, given Sullivan's repeated claims that he had left the sex industry behind, but Mitchelson suspects he had no choice. 'I think he was attracted to those people because they were people in his immediate financial circle. He didn't move in stockbroker circles so he wasn't going into the City for it. They were people with a lot of money that he was associated with so he went to them.'

In fact it was a rather better arrangement than the circumstances might suggest. The Golds provided several things that Sullivan could not and a synergy developed between them. They gave the *Sunday Sport* cheap offices at their Eagle Wharf Road depot, their company, Moore Harness, distributed the paper and they personally took half the risk. In exchange they got half the profits. The deal was struck on 16 May 1986 – David and Ralph Gold both became Apollo directors and each acquired 25 per cent of the new company. Mitchelson thought the Gold brothers got a great deal. 'I never knew what their financial commitment was but I guess it was guarantees rather than putting up funds. In the end very little money was spent, probably £75,000, but that's just a guess.'

The reason why so little money was spent on the *Sunday Sport* was a ruling by the Independent Broadcasting Authority, the body that controlled ITV. The IBA had become alarmed at the stories circulating about the proposed newspaper's sexually explicit content and the fact that three sex-industry bosses had combined to produce it. They decided to take no chances and banned the newspaper from advertising on both independent radio and television. It was a decision that Mitchelson thinks saved Sullivan and the Gold brothers a great deal of money. 'At the end of the day, because of the advertising ban by the television companies, we didn't spend most of the two million. The nearest estimate I could get was that we spent about £150,000 launching it, which was peanuts.'

The ban outraged David Sullivan for all sorts of reasons. It meant he had parted with 50 per cent of his company for no real reason. It seemed unfair that his newspaper had been judged and found wanting before it was actually produced. And, most worry-ingly of all, it threatened the success of the whole *Sunday Sport* project. Television advertising was considered crucial to what was, after all, a mass-market product.

Sullivan believes that the ban had more to do with his and the Golds' sex-industry background than with the *Sunday Sport* itself. He said at the time, 'They admit there's nothing wrong with the advert and a dummy run of the paper had eleven topless girls in it while a recent copy of another Sunday paper had twelve. It stinks of censorship and I'm furious.'[2]

Sullivan even went as far as challenging the IBA ban in the High Court, but without success. 'The ban on our adverts is a real body blow. I must admit I am really worried about the future but the paper will be out come hell or high water.'[3] The television ban has lasted until now. John Bull, the editor who later replaced Austin Mitchelson, also felt its effects, which he likened to 'fighting with one hand tied behind our back. All our rivals were advertising like mad. It was so unfair and we weren't allowed to advertise on radio either.'

The IBA ban was just the start of David Sullivan's problems. There was a string of protests as the launch date approached. Sullivan used to welcome this type of publicity but now he saw it as a distinctly two-edged sword. He worried that, while the paper was becoming better known, it might acquire a reputation of being unsuitable for a mass market and that could be a mortal blow. After all, newsagents had to be prepared to carry it on their counters, not on their top shelves, and national advertisers had to want to buy space in it.

Austin Mitchelson was particularly surprised by the vehemence of the opposition from other journalists. 'There was one group, the curiously named Campaign for Press and Broadcasting Freedom, who wanted to shut it down before they'd seen a copy. I guess that was because of the sex-industry background. I found it a little bit amazing that an organization which is battling for freedom wanted to prevent publication.'

Despite the intense opposition, the *Sunday Sport* was launched on 14 September 1986 and its lurid front page began a tradition of excess that continues to this day. The lead story was misleadingly headlined 'Charles sex romp shock' and included a picture of Prince Charles. In fact, the story had only the most spurious link with the Prince as it concerned an expedition organized by the charity Operation Raleigh, which 'turned into a sex romp'. Charles is the charity's patron but he knew nothing of the expedition. Alongside the main story was a full-colour picture of a busty blonde model, carefully cropped to make it looks as if she had some involvement in the lead story. The front page was finished off with a strapline informing the world that the paper had been 'banned by TV'. Page two contained no less than three sex stories, 'Sex beast still on the loose', 'Teenagers rape ordeal shock' and 'Smugglers bring in obscene videos'. The stories themselves were prurient enough but more worrying was their close proximity to another picture of a topless model. It was generally accepted practice in Fleet Street that sex stories were never juxtaposed with glamour pictures.

Despite the barrage of criticism, the *Sunday Sport*'s first editorial was triumphant in tone. Given all the objections it was an achievement simply to have made it to the news stands and Mitchelson couldn't resist the temptation to crow. 'They banned us from advertising on the box or even on radio. The so-called Big Boys of Fleet Street (well Wapping actually) tittered and scoffed. The editor of the *Daily Star* offered to bet money we would never come out. But here we are, fresh as paint and right as ninepence, bang on time.'[4]

One thing that distinguished the *Sunday Sport* from the rest of the Sunday papers was its pages of sexually explicit advertising. Sullivan always claims this element has been unfairly exaggerated, though he did once agree that the paper had more 'colour tits' than any other and even went on the record saying it would eventually 'out *Sun* the *Sun*'. One critic remarked that the *Sunday Sport*'s idea of editorial balance was to make sure its photographs showed both left and right breasts. Not surprisingly, the protests reached a peak immediately after the launch.

The National Union of Journalists' London Magazine Branch argued that the *Sunday Sport* wasn't a newspaper at all. They said its salaciousness coupled with its lack of real news meant that it could not even be compared to papers like the *News of the World*. The Magazine Branch Women's Committee called for it to be sold separately from other papers and kept away from children. Juliet Gosling told the *Guardian* forcibly, 'We don't want to ban *Sunday Sport*. We just want to get it classified as the crap that it is.'[5]

Within a couple of weeks the *Sunday Sport* had taken a further lurch downmarket. On 12 October the front page proclaimed 'We've girls, girls, girls' and inside the paper the number of topless pictures had virtually doubled. One page had no less than seven pairs of breasts on display. In the same edition was a bizarre article entitled 'Hands off boobs' which attempted to justify what was being done. It was written by a 'special correspondent'. The author was probably Mike Gabbert, the *Sunday Sport*'s executive editor and the man designated by Sullivan to take on the critics. He had previously worked for the *News of the World* and had even written an article about Sullivan in 1978 headlined 'Jail this vile beast'. No one was more surprised than Gabbert when Sullivan tracked him down and offered him the top job at the *Sunday Sport*.

Later Gabbert asked Sullivan what he had thought about the article but he simply laughed it off saying, 'I thought the piece was great.'[6]

Mike Gabbert had a reputation in Fleet Street as a tough street-fighter and he threw himself into the battle against the *Sunday Sport*'s critics. He went on the offensive, saying that no popular Sunday had real news any more and dismissing as 'spurious' claims that pictures of topless women lead to sex crimes. He even said the NUJ action was being led by the 'lank-haired, dirty-jeaned, feminist brigade'.[7] The arguments have continued to this day but they have not prevented the paper from building a substantial circulation.

The *Sunday Sport* planned what is known in the trade as a 'rolling launch'. Initially it would be sold only in London and the South East and would then work its way across the UK. Despite this reduced market the first four issues averaged a staggering 280,000 sales before settling down to a still very respectable 230,000. *Sunday Sport* staff were elated at a sensational start in the face of entrenched opposition, and the paper assumed the role of Fleet Street's *enfant terrible*.

Eddy Shah's *Today* newspaper was in trouble almost as quickly as Sullivan's *Sunday Sport* was in profit. Overburdened with debt and great expectations, Shah started to look round for a possible white knight. Mitchelson persuaded Sullivan that it would be a good idea to make a bid for *Today* as a publicity stunt. 'We decided that an attempt to buy it would get the name of our newspaper into other papers and on television. So one of my colleagues went round to the *Today* office with a cheque for ten million pounds and asked to see Eddy Shah and was basically shown the door. The Sunday version of *Today* was so appalling we'd always said the first thing we'd do would be to close it down anyway.' Predictably, the bogus offer attracted a large amount of media interest, as did a second stunt pulled just a few months later.

Sullivan had bought the old *Morning Star* building in Farringdon Road as a straightforward commercial proposition. But Mike Gabbert saw the opportunity to have some more fun and publicize the *Sunday Sport* at Fleet Street's expense. He told everyone that they were immediately launching a daily stable-mate from this new address. He said it would be just like the *Sunday Sport*, 'brash, raunchy, fun, bubbly and vulgar'. He then went on to terrify the other tabloid newspaper editors by saying, 'We are going for the readers of the other popular papers. I think the kind of paper we will be publishing will have an eventual natural circulation level of up to two million.'[8] In fact, David Sullivan sold the building just a few weeks later for a substantial profit but, for a moment, the whole of Fleet Street had held its breath. The *Daily Sport* would come – but not yet.

The *Sunday Sport* had not only performed better than *Today*. It had actually performed better than all of the other national newspapers launched at the same time. None of them could match it either financially or in numbers of readers. The *News on Sunday*, the *Sunday Correspondent* and *Sunday Today* all closed down within a few months and even the mighty *Independent on Sunday* has struggled to survive. Austin Mitchelson looks back with some pride at the *Sunday Sport*'s astonishing achievement. 'When I left, circulation was around 350,000 to 400,000 depending on which figures you use. It was also very successful in financial terms. It was trading at a profit from the second issue and earned back its investment within the first year. It was selling well, people were talking about it, people were laughing about it, people were enjoying it.'

Once the *Sunday Sport* had been established David Sullivan left his journalists to get on with it, much to Mitchelson's surprise. 'David was an arm's-length, even a bargepole-length, proprietor. I thought, because it was his idea to start the newspaper, he would be in the office interfering and saying do this, do that and don't do it any other way but my way. In fact I saw him once a week on a Tuesday morning at his home. He rarely came into the office and had little to say about what was going on in advance.'

Surprisingly, despite the successful launch of the *Sunday Sport*, Mitchelson lost his job after just five editions of the paper. A power struggle had developed between him and the irascible Mike Gabbert, his executive editor. Gabbert believed that Mitchelson's controversial editorial judgements were giving the paper's critics too much ammunition. He even told the *UK Press Gazette*, 'Austin was presented with a chance in a million and I am sorry he didn't grasp it in the way I expected him to.'[9]

The man appointed to replace Mitchelson was John Bull, an old Fleet Street hand and a friend of Mike Gabbert. Bull had spent eighteen years at the *News of the World* and he also believed it was Mitchelson's inexperience that had got the paper such a poor reputation so quickly. 'The early editions were a mishmash of court stories – rape cases and sex cases, badly edited. It takes a great deal of expertise to get it right and the editor didn't know how to do it. They were putting in all the wrong things. For example, they would run a rape case report next to a photograph of a topless model which would not get you any friends at all. It's a stupid thing to do. It also had the wrong kind of stories in the wrong places. It had page leads that should have been fillers and fillers that should have been page leads.'

John Bull and Mike Gabbert became the engine-room of the *Sunday Sport*, providing the editorial expertise they said it had previously lacked. Bull claims he altered the paper's mix of stories and toned down its salaciousness, though the individual changes were relatively minor. A typical Bull front page told the story of Tina Small, a model with an unbelievably large 84-inch bust. Alongside the full-colour picture was the headline '84 inch whopper – she's a nun'. The story began, 'Tina Small, the girl with the 84 inch whoppers, has given up sex – for ever.' It went on to claim that Ms Small had become a part-time nun.

Bull claims it is extremely difficult to find this type of racy human-interest story. The best ones are almost invariably sexy, humorous and must be just about credible. According to Bull it took months for the reporters to understand exactly what was required. 'Nobody would really believe that Tina would become a nun. But there was always that element that she might. Nobody would believe there was a bomber on the moon but well, it might be there. You've got to appreciate the subtlety of it. It's much more complex than it seems. What we were looking for was things that just might be true. It took a long time to explain to our staff and correspondents. They kept on missing the point and sending us horrific stories about cripples.'

David Sullivan revealed his own favourite *Sunday Sport* story in an interview with Lynn Barber. Predictably it was the one that sold the most. It was headlined 'Three stone woman lifts beauty crown' and was accompanied by a picture of a skeletal-looking female. 'We paid £3,500 for that story,' said Sullivan, 'which is quite a lot of money for us. But the editor fancied it and he was quite right because it sold 640,000 copies, which amazed me. It's a nice story too. She was anorexic and then went on to win the British gymnastic bodybuilding championships, so it shows people you can overcome it.'[10]

David Sullivan would often do more than just read the stories. John Bull remembers that he would come up with story ideas as well as more strategic suggestions to reduce criticism of the paper. 'He'd sometimes ring up and say there's such-and-such a story knocking about which he'd got from his contacts in the sex game. Other times he'd ring up and say; "I really want us to be anti-violence. I see our anti-violence stance as a way of justifying the pin-ups. Let's use some violent pictures like the burning ship in the Falklands and the one where the guy gets a bullet in the head in Vietnam and show how much nicer it is to see a girl topless." What Sullivan was getting at, and he's not a particularly articulate man, was trying to redefine obscenity in terms that are more meaningful. Let's tell our critics we're anti-war and anti-obscenity.'

These attempts to soften the criticisms were a little more noticeable away from the front page. Inside, the paper had reduced its coverage of prurient sex cases and introduced more human-interest stories such as a burglar haunted by a ghost, a court case involving a gardener who only wore gum boots and an ambulance-man whose dying road-accident victim turned out to be his mother. But, while some of the paper's more unsavoury elements may have gone, there were still plenty of things that people found offensive. Some seemed deliberately designed to shock. One Bull editorial attacked Liberace, the gay entertainer, who had just died. It began, 'Liberace was a dishonest old poof. Bent because he sued and took money off the *Mirror* for saying he was homosexual.' The leader concluded that his death from Aids was 'poetic justice'.

Traditionally the *Sunday Sport*'s greatest strength was its sports pages and particularly its coverage of football matches. Mitchelson had originally hired Bobby Moore, the former England soccer captain, as his sports editor and asked him to assemble a team of ex-professional footballers to report on the games they saw. It was a genuinely original idea but it took many months to realize its potential, as John Bull remembers:

'It was a great idea to have professional footballers rather than journalists commenting on matches. They'd done it on the telly and on the radio and now they were doing it for a newspaper. They'd phone in their comments, someone would take it down on a typewriter and the subs would go to work on it. The raw material was there but it needed tuning. The sub-editing talent and the tone were initially missing. It was a non-professional organization. The headlines weren't up to it. There was no hard, boiler-room, sub-editing experience to work with. We had to improve things a lot.'

Things were improved and, for a while, the sports reporting was actually quite good. But, with the *Sunday Sport*, the bizarre was never far away and this led to a number of increasingly heated confrontations between the sports staff and senior management. One early problem was the racing column supposedly written by Fred Archer, a jockey who had died over 100 years ago. It was entitled 'Tips from beyond the grave'. Some of the reporters felt that this type of column detracted from the otherwise very serious sports coverage. This essential contradiction was contained for almost two years primarily by the efforts of Tony Flood, the deputy sports editor, but it couldn't be controlled for ever. Events finally came to a head in early 1988 when David Sullivan appointed a new editor who started running front-page sports stories along the lines of 'Martians to invade Wimbledon' and, when nothing happened, 'Rain stops Martian invasion'. This nonsense finally destroyed the paper's one genuine area of excellence and led to the resignation of the entire sports department.

Another problem for John Bull was his discovery that the accounts department had been lagging behind with payments, a common practice with new businesses. One consequence of this was that many of the *Sunday Sport*'s freelance correspondents stopped writing for the paper, with predictably disastrous consequences. Bull was horrified when he finally discovered what was happening: 'The accounts staff were sitting on invoices for as long as they could and I had to point out to Dave that this was not always a good idea. We noticed there was a drying up of the flow of copy and we started to ask people what was going on and they said they weren't being paid. I said you can't treat correspondents like your 300 suppliers. We need to pay them up front.'

John Bull's resolution of this problem, coupled with the completion of the rolling launch in March 1987 and the lifting of the IBA radio ban, took the *Sunday Sport*'s weekly sales to over 500,000 and its readership to 1.5 million. In less than a year the paper had taken Britain by storm. Bull finally left the *Sunday Sport* in September 1987 following a family bereavement and Drew Robertson became the paper's third editor. Robertson came from a minor journalistic dynasty: his father had worked for *The Times* and his brother would later edit the *Daily Sport*.

Drew Robertson was always one of the stars of the *Sunday Sport*. He had worked on the paper since before its launch and was responsible for its truly innovative look and style. He was much younger than either Bull or Mitchelson and his appointment was something of a gamble for Sullivan, particularly since Mike Gabbert had just moved on to edit the *Daily Star* and would no longer be around to offer help and advice. Rab Anderson, the *Sunday Sport*'s former news editor, thought Drew Robertson was an inspired choice as editor: 'Robertson took the paper to its highest point. His layouts were extraordinary. They left far more experienced sub-editors gasping with amazement. He turned the paper into a cult.'

Robertson's front pages became the trade mark of the *Sunday Sport*. Huge headlines such as 'World War 2 bomber found on moon', coupled with sexy full-colour pin-ups cropped to give a 3D effect, made the paper a national talking point. John Bull agrees that Robertson deserves a lot – but not all – of the credit for this: 'Eddy Shah was talking a lot about breaking the mould but it was Drew who really did it. If you want to test that theory, look at the Sunday tabloid papers in 1986 and see what they look like today. They now look like early editions of *Sunday Sport*. But Drew didn't actually invent it. The *Sunday World* in Dublin were doing the same sort of thing. I don't know who their designer was but he was taking magazine techniques and applying them to newspapers which was not easy.'

One of Robertson's main changes as editor was to increase the emphasis on bizarre freak and alien stories. This was heralded by the *Sunday Sport*'s story on Jimmy Wrinkle, a man who lost thirty-six stone and was pictured on the front page holding acres of loose and wrinkled flesh. According to David Sullivan, 'It was the best-looking front page in my view. Everybody likes Jimmy Wrinkle; he's got a funny face. He's a character.'[11] Wrinkle was followed by other exclusives, such as 'Sex mad satanist stuffs girl into Sunday roast' and 'One in seven people is a space alien', written by the ubiquitous Bertie Ollocks. Drew Robertson justified the use of such fanciful stories to the *Guardian* newspaper in 1988. He said, 'There must be something else out there in the universe and certain sections of the public think it's aliens . . . If some woman is willing to tell you down the phone she had sex with an alien, it's worth recounting to your readers.'[12]

It was a sentiment that an increasing number of readers seemed to accept, and not just working-class readers. According to Robertson, 'It's no longer your out-of-work labourer. It's your city gent, your city whiz-kid, who find *Sunday Sport* fun and a laugh. I think most of our readers laugh with *Sunday Sport* as opposed to at it. A lot of the alien-type UFO stories are created by readers writing in and telling us about them.'[13]

But one area of the *Sunday Sport* that had become less and less humorous was the increasing number of sexually explicit advertisements. John Bull was just one senior staffer who had opposed the paper's sex contact ads and been pleased when they started to decline in popularity. Unfortunately, this coincided with the launch of telephone-sex chatlines, and adverts such as 'Randy company director looking for bored housewives' were replaced with even less palatable messages offering men the opportunity to 'Spurt in my face' and 'Cream my big tits'.

Not all of the *Sunday Sport*'s staff objected to the adverts, however. Drew Robertson was prepared to defend them. He told the *Guardian*, 'I think they are probably harmless. They are aimed at adults and adults probably read them.'[14] But they caused Austin Mitchelson, the first editor of *Sunday Sport*, finally to give up on the paper: 'I don't look at the *Sunday Sport* now. I've seen copies and I wouldn't bring it home because of its contents. What has changed are the telephone-sex lines which didn't exist at the time *Sunday Sport* was launched. Apparently David Sullivan is now in that business and those adverts tend to be fairly salacious. Page after page of that tends to set the tone for everything else.'

Another area of controversy within the paper was the use of editorial space for advertising purposes. John Bull remembers Sullivan often asking him to promote his products. Bull argued that this would undermine the readers' confidence in the paper. 'He used to try and get me to run things he was selling as editorials and I used to say, "No, you'll destroy the credibility of the paper."'

After Bull left, David Sullivan finally got his own way. A series of features were run using *Sunday Sport* models to promote two 'miracle' slimming aids, Speedslim and Figureform. These were being advertised by Tobyward and Quietlynn respectively and sold in the Private Shop chain. The *Sunday Times* tried to ask Brian Richards about Figureform but his 'administrator', Christine King, said, 'He won't talk to you. While he doesn't want to appear uncooperative, when you have been misquoted as many times as he has you get wary.'[15] Speedslim was eventually condemned by both the Office of Fair Trading and the Advertising Standards Authority for making extravagant claims. They haven't yet ruled on Figureform but, as the *Sunday Times* revealed, far from being a 'miracle' potion it contained little more than peas, beans and lentils.

A third area of complaint related to the way in which the *Sunday Sport* obtained and published some of its more sensational stories. Robertson's determination to get scoops was starting to get the paper into serious trouble with the Press Council, the industry's watch-dog body. It culminated with his pursuit of a story involving Gordon Kaye, the star who played René in the BBC's *'Allo 'Allo* TV programme. On 25 January 1990 Kaye was involved in a major car crash. For three days he was kept on a life-support machine at London's Charing Cross Hospital. His condition was closely monitored by the tabloid press, all eager for news. Robertson, like many other editors, despatched reporters to the hospital, but they were not content to prepare background reports and wait until Kaye was well enough to be interviewed. Instead, the *Sunday Sport* team decided to ignore the instructions of the medical staff and secretly entered Kaye's room, photographed him and even attempted an interview. As soon as staff realized what was happening the team was thrown out but, by then, the *Sunday Sport* had its story.

Drew Robertson was proud of this scoop. He had obtained a story that the whole of Fleet Street wanted, and had done so for virtually nothing. The fact that the methods involved were completely unethical and may have jeopardized Kaye's recovery do not appear to have even been considered. Gordon Kaye's agent made a desperate effort to get a High Court injunction preventing publication but failed, forcing Lord Justice Glidewell to conclude reluctantly: 'It is well known in English law that there is no right of privacy, and accordingly there is no right of action for breach of a person's privacy.' However, the judge did go on to suggest that Parliament might wish to consider whether the law should be changed to protect the privacy of an individual, an idea that continues to be vigorously debated today.

The *Sunday Sport* eventually published both the Gordon Kaye pictures and the so-called 'interview' in a colour special on 4 March. The paper was forced to confess, on its front page, that the bedside shots were actually no more than 'sneak' pictures. It then went on to try and justify itself by claiming that the story was intended to reassure millions of *'Allo 'Allo* fans, and even spuriously suggested that the whole affair raised questions of censorship, saying, 'This is the picture you nearly didn't see – brave *'Allo 'Allo* star Gordon Kaye recovering from surgery.' The piece admitted that *Sunday Sport* newsmen had sneaked to the 48-year-old actor's bedside, that the pictures had been taken without Kaye's consent and that he hadn't agreed to an interview. But, despite all this, Sport Newspapers still tried to copyright the article by parodying the BBC's script and writing, 'Listen very carefully, we will say this only once. Nick this and you will be making a very big booby.'[16]

The 'scoop' provoked several debates in the House of Commons on the standards of the tabloid press and caused a public mood swing against stunts of this kind. Kaye is a popular, likeable figure and it had clearly been a crass and stupid thing to do. According to one MP, it meant 'the press are now drinking in the last-chance saloon'.

The number of complaints received by the Press Council about the *Sunday Sport* continued to grow under Robertson's editorship. The Press Council advised newsagents that the *Sunday Sport*'s claim to be a family newspaper was 'absurd' and that it should not be displayed alongside newspapers but on higher shelves with other soft porno-graphy. They also ruled that Robertson's threat to publish the telephone number of a complainant who had suggested that the *Sunday Sport* was racist was completely irresponsible.

This was all more than Robertson could take. He published an extraordinary editorial entitled 'Bollocks to the Press Council' and subtitled '*Sunday Sport* leaps to defend your freedom'. The piece, signed by Robertson himself, began, 'We're pretty thick skinned 'ere at Scumbag towers (*Sunday Sport*'s HQ). But there comes a time when you've gotta deliver a swift kick in the bollocks to the killjoys in life. Cutting the bullshit it's about time the Press Council were Press Councilled. In its findings against *Sunday Sport* I, as Editor, am accused of threatening behaviour. OUTRAGEOUS. I am also racist. COBBLERS.' The editorial then rambled on a little before finally concluding, '*Sunday Sport* represents you, we're proud of you and reflect your attitudes. But we will not take a heap of shit from trumped up newspaper bashers whose sole aim is to wet nurse the public and curtail our greatest British asset . . . FREEDOM.'[17]

Shortly after this latest episode David Sullivan decided to replace Robertson and appointed Ian Pollack as the new editor. But Robert-son's departure marked the end of an era for the *Sunday Sport*. Its *enfant terrible* days were gone. Pollack's job was primarily to be one of consolidation.

Ian Pollack edited the *Sunday Sport* for almost four years. Initially his Fleet Street experience allowed him to stem the fall in circula-tion that had begun under Drew Robertson, but the economic downturn meant it was a losing battle. Sullivan used this decline in circulation as a justification to start interfering with the *Sunday Sport*. He insisted on seeing the front page in advance of publica-tion and would often override Pollack's judgement on both its layout and content. According to Pollack, 'He saw *Sunday Sport* as his paper. *Sunday Sport* was David Sullivan. David Sullivan was *Sunday Sport*. One of the reasons why I finally quit as editor was that I was sick to the back teeth with the interference of David Sullivan.'

Pollack may have presided over a gently diminishing readership but *Sunday Sport* had still been a tremendous success. During Apollo Ltd.'s first three years it had become an immensely profitable business for David Sullivan and his two silent partners. The 1989 accounts showed a healthy profit of £304,000 which increased in 1990 to over £900,000 though no dividend was paid. But, as with many sets of accounts, the real story is not in the profit-and-loss statement but in the notes that accompany it.

Note thirteen reveals the true situation: it is entitled 'Transactions involving directors.' In 1989 Roldvale, David Sullivan's master company, received £500,000 in consultancy fees. The previous year it had received £335,000. Note thirteen also shows that in 1989 two Gold-brother companies, Ann Summers (Sales) Ltd. and Petbridge Ltd., received no less than £700,000 in consultancy fees. Had all these fees been retained in the company, profits would have increased from £300,000 to £1.3 million for the year – not bad for an investment of just £150,000.

There was one other financial transaction of real significance during Apollo's first three years of trading. On 14 August 1987 a new director, Mr Andrew Cameron, was appointed to the board and a new shareholder appeared on the Register of Members: United Newspapers, publishers of the *Daily Express* and *Daily Star*, had purchased 25 per cent of the company.

NOTES

1. *World in Action*, 21 September 1992.
2. *Ilford Recorder*, 21 August 1986.
3. Ibid.
4. *Sunday Sport*, 14 September 1986.
5. *Guardian*.
6. *Evening Standard*, 7 September 1987.
7. *Guardian*.
8. *The Times*, 2 September 1987.
9. *UK Press Gazette*, 6 October 1986.
10. *Independent on Sunday* 27 May 1990.
11. Ibid.
12. *Guardian*, 12 December 1988.
13. Ibid.
14. Ibid.

15. *Sunday Times*, 8 September 1991.
16. *Sunday Sport*, 4 March 1990.
17. *Sunday Sport*, 18 November 1991.

CHAPTER SEVEN

THE LOST WEEKEND

The 'Lost Weekend' is the name given by senior staff at Express Newspapers to the eight turbulent weeks when David Sullivan controlled the *Daily Star*, the distinctly downmarket sister of the *Daily Express*. During this brief period Britain's national newspapers could, for the first time, be divided into not two but three separate categories: the qualities, the tabloids and what became known as the 'bonks'. It was to be one of the most interesting and controversial periods in Fleet Street's recent history.

Lord Stevens, chairman of Express Newspapers' holding company, United Newspapers, thought long and hard before linking up with David Sullivan and the *Sunday Sport*: United Newspapers controlled not only the *Express* and *Star* but also the *Yorkshire Post* and *Punch* magazine. Stevens knew that any deal he made was bound to be criticized but the *Daily Star* was in a near-terminal condition. It was losing money fast and the position would deteriorate even further if Sullivan fulfilled his pledge and launched a daily version of the *Sunday Sport*. Stevens believed that by acquiring a minority stake in Apollo Ltd., the company that owned the *Sunday Sport*, he could prevent this from happening and get Fleet Street's newest whiz-kids to help revitalize his ailing paper into the bargain.

It was United Newspapers' own fault that the *Daily Star* had got into such a state. It was originally conceived as a cheap and cheerful way of utilizing spare *Daily Express* printing capacity and, at the same time, moving into the *Sun*'s highly profitable market. Unfortunately, United got the sums all wrong. Despite their substantial experience in newspaper production and the advantages offered by the economies of scale involved, the *Daily Star* made a loss from the very beginning, and by the summer of 1987 this loss had reached over £1 million a month.

Staff morale was also at rock bottom following the payment of several sizeable legal bills, the most well known of which resulted from the Jeffrey Archer libel settlement. The paper had wrongly accused Archer of consorting with a prostitute and paid him £500,000 in compensation.

United Newspapers were not the only company interested in doing a deal with David Sullivan following the spectacular success of the *Sunday Sport*. Another major Fleet Street publisher held two secret meetings with Sullivan and Mike Gabbert at Claridge's and the Savoy. He was so concerned that his reputation might be damaged if news of the talks leaked out that he asked Sullivan and Gabbert to conceal their true identities. They ended up using the unlikely pseudonyms of Mr Smith and Mr Jones.

Given the furtive attitude of the competition, it is not surprising that it was Lord Stevens who finally clinched the deal. At the time it seemed an elegant solution to the *Daily Star*'s problems. Mike Gabbert, the editorial director of the *Sunday Sport*, would become the *Daily Star*'s new editor on a salary of £100,000. David Sullivan would become its special consultant. The *Sunday Sport* would become its stepsister and, best of all, Sullivan agreed not to launch a *Daily Sport* provided United did not attempt a *Sunday Star*.

In return for all this, United Newspapers would spend £2 million on a 24.8 per cent stake in Apollo Ltd. and pay an extra 0.5 pence for every copy of the *Daily Star* sold above the January–June average of 1.3 million per day. United would also help Apollo to improve its marketing techniques in the face of the IBA ban and give advice on how to attract more legitimate advertising. To this end David Sullivan even agreed to tone down the *Sunday Sport*. It looked as though there was something in the deal for everyone.

David Buchan was the *Daily Star*'s pugnacious leader writer at the time. He remembers being taken aback at just how pleased United's management were with the *Sunday Sport* link-up, particularly given its bizarre reputation. 'I know in my own local pub that we had a copy just to find out what had happened to the London bus that had landed on the moon. We were falling over ourselves over our lunchtime pints it was so gross. But they felt they could make money because the *Sunday Sport* was remarkably successful whereas the *Star* was losing money. They decided that if they got the two together and ran them seven days, they saw the prospect of it becoming a decent commercial venture.'

But it was not only United's management that were pleased with the outcome. David Sullivan was also very happy, albeit for different reasons. He said at the time, 'I'm pleased we did a deal with Express Newspapers because with them it was upfront and open. We went to their offices as ourselves. With the others it was like something out of a James Bond film.'[1] In many ways this deal represented the ultimate accolade for Sullivan. The establishment had not only asked for his help but had paid handsomely for the privilege. In a very bullish interview he told the *UK Press Gazette*, 'It's a challenge to me, a game. But it's a game I'm going to win.' He went on to explain that he wanted to break Rupert Murdoch's stranglehold on the British press. 'That's the master plan. I'm proud to be British and it needles me that half the industry is owned by an Australian. The *Star* is out to steal the *Sun*'s readers and the *Sunday Sport* wants some of the *News of the World*.'[2]

Sullivan was obviously cock-a-hoop with the deal. It really was an astonishing achievement, particularly bearing in mind that he had been publishing a national newspaper for only twelve months. In another upbeat interview, allegedly from his bath, Sullivan told the *Financial Times*, 'The battle now starts. What we have achieved until now is nothing. My aim is to punch a big hole in Mr Rupert Murdoch's newspapers.'[3]

Mike Gabbert followed his master and also climbed aboard the anti-Murdoch bandwagon, though a little more cautiously. 'I'm not going to say we're going to beat the *Sun* in a circulation war,' he said. 'What I'm saying is that I will get the *Star* to a circulation of two million and after that United Newspapers will have to think about pouring in a great deal of money, millions and millions, in order to go from there. That I think is an achievable figure, the rest depends on the depth of the purse because TV advertising is very expensive. The *Sun* spends fortunes on it and we will have to match their spending.'[4]

Away from all the hype, the deal looked very strange indeed. The *Daily Star* and the *Sunday Sport* had been sniping at each other for months. Alix Palmer, the *Daily Star*'s women's editor, had repeatedly criticized the use of topless pin-ups in the tabloid press and had been attacked for her pains by Mike Gabbert in his *Sunday Sport* column. Just before the two papers linked up he wrote, 'They must be a rum lot at the *Daily Star*. No wonder it's shedding circulation like falling leaves. First its editor, Lloyd Turner, offers on radio to bet money that *Sunday Sport* will never appear ... And now their women's editor, Alix Palmer, calls for a ban on topless pin-ups. Perhaps she's been sucked in by the nonsense put about by the loonier fringes of Women's Lib, who claim that seeing a pretty girl no more unclothed than on a holiday beach makes men into slobbering fiends.'[5]

Not surprisingly, given this sort of attack, the *Daily Star* staff were a little concerned about having Mike Gabbert as their new boss. Gabbert, however, did his best to reassure everyone, at least about their jobs: 'I'm not coming in here with an axe. Anyone who did that at a paper with a 1.25 million circulation would be mad. There are some highly talented people in here, though they may have been underused in the past. My message to the staff is that there are no sinister shades behind this deal. It's going to be a fun partnership. We are going upwards and onwards from here.'[6]

Mike Gabbert's idea of 'upwards and onwards' soon became very clear indeed. His first act was to wrestle a crate of Whitbread beer up to his office and offer it as a reward for the best headline of the week. It was rumoured to have been won by a sub-editor working on a story about a gay footballer at Glasgow Celtic. The resulting caption had a directness that appealed to the new editor: it simply said 'POOFS' in 144-point type accompanied by a picture of the Glasgow Celtic badge.

If the caption competition hinted at the paper's new style, the editorial conferences confirmed the journalists' worst fears. Gabbert's first instruction set the tone: henceforth, the paper should carry two sets of 'the biggest boobs possible' in every edition.[7] It was a shift in policy that horrified Charles Wintour, a former director of Express Newspapers: 'I think it's absolutely appalling. I think it's a prostitution of journalism. I think to elevate boobs over the prospect of a major war involving the West in the Gulf is really crazy. I think it gives the British public an extremely false impression of what's important in the world and I think that journalists should have absolutely nothing to do with it. If you want to produce a fun paper, OK, but don't call it a newspaper and don't employ journalists to do it. Employ fiction writers.'[8]

In September 1987, as every *Sunday Sport* reader knew, 'the biggest boobs possible' belonged to young Natalie Banus. Natalie was a fifteen-year-old schoolgirl who had been featured in a number of peekaboo articles in the *Sunday Sport*, and Gabbert lost no time in introducing her to the *Daily Star*. She appeared on the front page within twenty-four hours of his taking control of the paper, alongside the caption, 'She's 15, she's got a forty-inch bust, she's going topless in 34 days. If you were her Mum, would you let her?' *Daily Star* readers were then invited to write in and vote on the issue.

Alix Palmer hit back two days later in her own column, under the headline, 'Mum, you should be ashamed'. Palmer wrote, 'At the tender age of fifteen when little girls should still be talking to their dolls, Natalie Banus is posing for sexy pictures. Her Mum, Gill, says, if you've got it flaunt it. Maybe so. But I say not when you are under-aged and too under-experienced to know the ways of the wicked world. My view is that Mum should be ashamed of herself.'[9]

But Palmer was comprehensively outgunned by her editor. The same day that Palmer's article appeared, Mike Gabbert gave over almost the whole of pages two and three to a busty schoolgirl spread headlined 'Big is boobiful'. Alongside several pictures captioned 'Gymslip girls are busting out' he wrote, 'Britain's schools are bursting at the seams with budding beauties who have done their homework and found that BIG equals BEAUTIFUL. And that's good news for all the shops that supply navy blue knickers, gymslips and blazers.'[10] This civil war continued on the *Daily Star* for several weeks. Palmer became increasingly angry about Gabbert's obsession with proliferating 'pairs', as the nipple count was called. But this was just the start of the *Daily Star*'s dramatic plunge downmarket, as Palmer revealed to Thames Television's *This Week* programme. She said, 'In conference this morning he went through parts of the paper and eventually came to my Agony Column and said in future he wanted much shorter and raunchier letters about how my husband is tearing my sister's knickers off and that sort of thing. And I said with a sort of half laugh, "We don't get too many letters like that, Mike," and he said, "Come on Alix, I've never come across an Agony Aunt yet who used real letters." So I said, "Well I'm sorry, I won't make them up." He turned to one of his associate editors and said, "Get me someone in here by next week who will."'[11]

The Agony Column was passed to Moira Petty, a *Daily Star* features writer, and raunchily retitled 'Nothing shocks Moira'. Petty, too, was left in no doubt as to the sort of page Gabbert wanted: 'It was to be very different from the old column, full of very sexually explicit letters. That was to be the only subject we covered and when I asked him what kind of letters he said they should be a masturbatory device for readers. He didn't say make them up but he did say he wanted them quickly and they were to appear from somewhere. And there weren't any lying around in the office.'[12]

Petty, like Palmer, decided to resign soon after Gabbert listed his new requirements for the Agony Column, but it wasn't her only reason for quitting. 'That was just one indicator as to where the paper was going,' Petty explained. 'I gave it a week, I looked at the paper very carefully every day and I was shocked at the way the paper had changed entirely. There was no real writing, intelligence or wit. I also really hated the way that women were portrayed in the paper, they were these chauvinist playthings divested of clothes and dignity.'[13]

David Sullivan and Mike Gabbert were not in the least bit deterred by the negative reactions of some of the journalists and stuck rigidly to their game plan. The number of topless pictures in the *Daily Star* doubled while the news stories halved. Sullivan then began aggressively cross promoting the two papers and even went as far as renaming the *Sunday Sport* the *Star Sunday Sport*. According to David Buchan the atmosphere changed almost overnight: 'As soon as Mike Gabbert walked into the office the impact was there straight away, both in the design style of the paper and the actual writing content. We used to have good arguments about fairly serious things because the *Star* had a funny formula of a lot of froth and entertainment but the other part, which I used to call the fig-leaf department, would discuss more serious political and social issues at some length. When the Sullivan regime came in we were immediately trying to find two-headed grannies on the moon.'

Buchan was convinced that Gabbert was always working to Sullivan's agenda, even though Sullivan rarely interfered with individual stories. They did, however, talk constantly on the telephone and Sullivan inundated Gabbert's office with faxes. Buchan remembers one story in particular that got spiked simply because Gabbert thought Sullivan might object to it: 'We were preparing a very major series on jiggery pokery at the race-track, illegal payments etc., to coincide with the Lester Piggott case. In the course of this research we kept coming across friends of David Sullivan, who is a well-known racehorse owner. When the Piggott trial came up we were told to drop the subject because it wasn't something in which *Star* readers would be interested, which I found quite extraordinary since the *Star* prides itself on its racing coverage and reckons to be very widely read by punters.'

A few years later David Sullivan wrote an article in the *Independent Magazine* that seems to cast some light on this curious incident. It claims to be a tribute to Lester Piggott, but parts of it have a strongly autobiographical feel. Perhaps Gabbert realized just how closely Sullivan identified with the imprisoned Piggott. Sullivan wrote:

> I greatly admire how Lester stood up to perhaps his greatest challenge of all – his conviction in 1987 for defrauding the Inland Revenue. Lester had spent his life revelling in public acclaim and was completely hooked on it. The humiliation of prison must have been devastating and far harder to accept than any financial penalty.
>
> But Lester survived. He wrapped himself in a prison-issue jacket, he pushed his prison-issue wheelbarrow and he led a prison-issue life. But, in Lester's case, there were packs of journalists and photographers behind every gate and every spot-light. Some of the stories that the press wrote about him were disgraceful: he was dying, he was having visits whenever he wanted, he was even leading a life of luxury. I've been in prison myself and I know for a fact that people don't lead lives of luxury behind bars.
>
> The establishment treated Lester badly over his tax problems and throughout his professional life he has never got the attention he deserves. Maybe people take jockeys for granted – they were once considered rather socially inferior and, unlike top boxers, jockeys work every day and don't just appear for two or three grand occasions each year. Or maybe it's because Lester is small

and nobody could ever call him a warm, likeable or well-spoken person.

In Britain we look down on winners. We like losers – such as the disastrous ski jumper Eddie the Eagle, or Frank Bruno, who goes to America and gets himself battered to shreds for four or five rounds. When we have a real world-class champion sportsman like Lester Piggott we clap him in the slammer.[14]

Gabbert's decision to spike the racing investigation occurred at the same time as the result of the Natalie Banus poll was announced. In fact, the poll was academic as the pictures had already been taken, but that was not the end of the Natalie Banus story. The *Daily Star* had also given a titillating account of how she had been molested by a boy and supposedly enjoyed part of the assault. It was not true and Ian Mayhew, the features editor, decided to delete that part of the story. 'I took those references out but they still appeared in the newspaper the following day because the editor specifically wanted those pieces in.' For Mayhew this was the last straw: 'It's become a newspaper that I can't take home because I have two young children. And to be features editor of a paper that you can't take home is unacceptable to me which is why I've resigned.'[15]

David Buchan had also become disenchanted with the paper. His leader articles, while written in a tabloid style, often dealt with fairly complex subjects yet he was being given less and less space by Mike Gabbert. 'I was originally writing leaders that would be about 300 to 500 words every day. These were then hacked down to about five sentences. At the time, on a word for word basis, I reckon I became the highest paid journalist on Fleet Street because I ended up only doing about 100 words a day. Life became extremely tedious. Any features I wrote that were even semi-serious were a waste of time, they weren't interested.' Buchan got to a point when he couldn't keep his frustration bottled up any more. At a Labour Party fringe meeting in Brighton he referred to the new downmarket *Daily Star* as 'a soft-porn rag'. He was sacked the following day, but he was not the only one prepared to speak out publicly.

Alix Palmer, the former women's editor, forcefully pointed out the likely consequences of the *Daily Star*'s plunge into the gutter. 'The *Sun* is going to have to go even further downmarket, because they'll have to compete. And even the wonderful *Daily Mirror* is going to have to go downmarket, and that would be disastrous. There is almost nothing in the *Star* these days which tells you what happened in the world yesterday. And I think if you're going to ask what a newspaper is, it's about what happened yesterday, and that's not the *Star*.'[16]

But it was not only journalists who were protesting. Some members of the public became so horrified at the remorseless march downmarket that they decided to take matters into their own hands. A bogus police letter was sent to dozens of Leeds newsagents saying that 'retailers found displaying, advertising or visually promoting *Star Sunday Sport* within view of minors will face criminal charges'. It should have been instantly recognized as a hoax but with the *Sport/Star* link-up almost anything was possible.

By now the pressure on United Newspapers was becoming intense. Questions were asked in Parliament about the recent events at the *Daily Star*. Lord Stevens initially defended the paper, claiming that critics had exaggerated the changes and describing it as still 'a good read'. He also defended his editor, Mike Gabbert, saying, 'He's a lot of fun. You can feel there's a great amount of electricity there.' But even Stevens was forced to admit there was too much bonking, though he added, 'Bonking, as I understand it, is now in the Oxford Dictionary.'[17]

While Lord Stevens may have been prepared to give the new-look *Daily Star* the benefit of the doubt, the advertisers were not. Some of them had become very uneasy about being identified with such a controversial product. Tesco, the supermarket giant, publicly cancelled a £400,000 advertising contract with the paper. A spokesman for Tesco told the *Sunday People* at the time, 'We wouldn't want to be seen to be connected with the *Star* in its current form. We feel it's not the sort of thing our family-type customers would read and see no value in advertising in the paper. A large majority of our staff, some 80 per cent in fact, are women and the way the *Star* portrays women, I think, insults them.'[18]

Tesco was not alone in reconsidering its contracts. The chief executive of Woolworths, Geoffrey Mulchay, said, 'We are reviewing the situation. We certainly don't like the change of policy at the *Star*.'[19] They were swiftly followed by Sainsbury and Harris Furnishings. Now it was the turn of David Sullivan and Mike Gabbert to start feeling uneasy.

David Buchan believes that the Express team was naïve about David Sullivan: 'I don't think the management of Express Newspapers realized what Sullivan was going to do to the *Star* as a product. I think they felt he might have tinkered a bit with it but not the revolution and the headlong plunge downwards, I don't think they expected that. I think it took them by surprise.'

Andrew Cameron, the United Newspapers executive on Apollo's board of directors, later told the Monopolies and Mergers Commission that he and Lord Stevens had tried desperately to reduce the 'sleaze' element being introduced into the paper but to no avail. The MMC report summed up Cameron's comments in this way:

> Mr Cameron told us that while Mr Gabbert had indicated a willingness to comply with these instructions he had not in fact done so. Mr Cameron attributed this to contrary advice and pressure which he believed Mr Gabbert was at the time receiving daily from Mr Sullivan on the picture and editorial content of the paper. We put to Mr Cameron Mr Sullivan's view that Mr Gabbert was a strong-willed independent editor unwilling to take advice from anyone. Mr Cameron said that was not his experience and that Mr Gabbert had told him he was taking advice from Mr Sullivan.[20]

United Newspapers began to view their link with David Sullivan as nothing short of disastrous. Mike Gabbert's plunge downmarket was mirrored only by the fall in circulation – within a few weeks circulation was down by 250,000. The threat of a substantial loss of advertising was the final straw. After just eight weeks United Newspapers decided unilaterally to end their agreement with Apollo and Lord Stevens himself decided to break the bad news. He took Mike Gabbert to lunch at the Savoy and listed in turn the problems of falling sales, declining advertising and increasingly hostile criticism. Finally he leaned back, lit a big cigar and delivered the *coup de grâce*. 'Mike,' he said, 'I thought I could live with it. But I can't. I want a divorce.'

The separation, though, would come too late. The damage was already done, and it would take several years for the *Daily Star* to recover. Brian Hitchen, the current editor, told the MMC that he did not believe the newspaper would have survived had it not been for the massive financial resources of the United Newspapers group.

David Sullivan was outraged at the behaviour of United. He immediately warned them that he intended to take legal action over what he saw as an unwarranted breach of the agreement. He told the *Independent* that he was shell shocked: 'It wasn't cricket. Lord Stevens has still not rung me. It's not really good enough. In my own way I am very much an Englishman and a very straight and honest person. I'm sad they have not behaved as Englishmen should. It could end up with an embittered legal battle.'[21] In fact, United Newspapers and Apollo quickly came to an understanding. United agreed to return their shares for nothing and pay substantial compensation, thus writing off a £2 million investment in just eight weeks. It may have been a PR disaster for Sullivan but financially it was the deal of a lifetime.

David Buchan, now a freelance journalist, looks back on the 'lost weekend' as something of a tragedy for the *Daily Star*. 'Sullivan's effect on the *Star* was disastrous. It had little to do with what I regard as proper, legitimate journalism. It was pandering to some pretty low tastes. I think Express Newspapers continues to suffer to this day because, whilst it was only for a few weeks that Sullivan ruled the *Star*, it did immense damage.'

Peter Grimsditch, the first editor of the *Daily Star* and later the editor of the *Daily Sport*, thought the disastrous collapse of the venture was, in retrospect, all too predictable. 'The changes that were made in the *Daily Star* were too abrupt. It was too much too soon and the readers couldn't take it, the Express management couldn't take it and some of the advertisers couldn't take it either. It would have worked much better if they'd spent twelve months doing what they did in twelve days.'

NOTES

1. *UK Press Gazette*, 7 September 1987.
2. Ibid.
3. *Financial Times*, 4 September 1987.

4. *This Week*, Thames Television, 1 October 1987.
5. *Sunday Sport*, 2 August 1987.
6. *UK Press Gazette*, 7 September 1987.
7. Ibid.
8. *This Week*, 1 October 1987.
9. *Daily Star*, 9 September 1987.
10. Ibid.
11. *This Week*, 1 October 1987.
12. Ibid.
13. Ibid.
14. *Independent Magazine*, 27 October 1990.
15. *This Week*, 1 October 1987.
16. Ibid.
17. *Guardian*, 10 October 1987.
18. *Sunday People*, 4 October 1987.
19. Ibid.
20. MMC report on David Sullivan and the BEP, 4 May 1990.
21. *Independent*, 31 October 1987.

CHAPTER EIGHT

MEDIA MOGUL

The collapse of the *Daily Star/Sunday Sport* link hurt David Sullivan's pride more than his wallet and he was determined to take revenge. He knew that, while he could no longer join Express Newspapers, he could certainly compete with them and perhaps even beat them in a circulation war.

In August 1988 Sullivan began a rolling launch of the *Daily Sport*, the paper which Express Newspapers said it feared most of all. Initially it was published only on Wednesdays but, as circulation grew, it was made available on Fridays, then Saturdays, and finally went daily in late 1990. The fact that Sullivan and his two partners did not have to invest any additional money in the new paper simply proved the tremendous profitability of their earlier operations.

After some discussions, Peter Grimsditch was invited to be the *Daily Sport*'s first editor. He found that Sullivan was genuinely bitter at the way he had been treated by Express Newspapers and was surprised to find himself developing some sympathy for his new boss. 'I think it's no secret that David was very upset by the collapse in 1988 of what was almost a joint venture with the *Express*. He is honest to the point of being boring and I think if Express Newspapers were unaware of whom they were going into partnership with then my big question would be "Who's running the *Express*?" not "What's wrong with Sport Newspapers?" At the end of it I think he was determined to say, "Right, if you think I'm not good enough for you then fine, I'll do my own thing," and essentially the birth of the *Daily Sport* is an attempt to replace the *Daily Star*.'

Peter Grimsditch has worked on most of Fleet Street's tabloid newspapers and is liked throughout the industry. His background is certainly unusual for a tabloid editor: he graduated from Oriel College, Oxford, with a double first in classics, so single-handedly destroying the myth that they are all uneducated hacks who know and that if it were on the bottom shelf children would be able get hold of it, whereas if it were on the top shelf with magazines like *Penthouse* and the like, that was the proper place for that kind of material.'

Sir Louis also believes the Press Council were right at the time to have applied their comments equally to both the *Daily Sport* and *Sunday Sport*. However, he does accept that there was an improvement in the *Daily Sport* under the editorship of Peter Grimsditch: 'I think society to some extent must assist in the process of protecting children against material which is unsuitable. Looking at the *Daily Sport* in 1989/90 when I was at the Press Council, I would have thought it was unsuitable. Looking at it more recently, I'm not at all sure that would be the judgement I would make.'

Despite the Press Council's continual criticism of his newspapers, David Sullivan remained as determined as ever to become a press baron and have his revenge on Express Newspapers. With the *Sunday Sport* firmly established and the *Daily Sport*'s rolling launch well under way he started to look round for other media targets. In an unusually modest interview with Ray Snoddy of the *Financial Times* he said, 'I've been playing non-league football as a newspaper publisher. I want to get into the second or third division and maybe one day the first division.'[2] He then announced that he had bought a 5 per cent stake in the Portsmouth and Sunderland newspaper group, a company that had originally printed the *Sunday Sport* before it switched to a more lucrative contract with the *Observer* newspaper.

Sullivan was pleased with his new acquisition and happily confided his secret for recognizing a winning investment: 'I look at dozens of companies every week. I just look at the company's accounts. You must look at the assets. Not the book assets but the real brand assets and at the freeholds, particularly when it was last valued.' He then went on to claim that the Portsmouth and Sunderland's value 'shone out like a glowing light'. He said that its assets included three evening newspapers, four paid-for weeklies, twelve free newspapers, stakes in radio stations, modern printing presses, forty-eight newsagents and convenience stores, before you even talk about freeholds and all for not much more than the £25 million no better. Grimsditch owed his job on the *Daily Sport* to the intervention of David and Ralph Gold, the co-owners of Apollo Ltd. (which was about to be renamed Sport Newspapers). It was one of the few occasions on which they had ever directly interfered with the day-to-day running of the paper. David Sullivan had originally planned to fill the post with an internal appointment but the Gold brothers insisted that a more experienced man was needed, and Grimsditch was the obvious choice.

A number of journalists at Sport Newspapers feared that this intervention, coupled with the recent *Daily Star* débâcle, meant the Gold brothers intended to take a much more active role on the paper. But, according to Peter Grimsditch, they continued to keep a low profile. Looking back on his editorship he said, 'I suppose I talk to Ralph two or three times a year and that's all. I think that he would be far more concerned with what goes on if we started losing money and, as we don't lose money, he leaves us to get on with it.'

David Sullivan, though, certainly wasn't ready to let Grimsditch simply get on with it. He never came to the *Daily Sport*'s new Manchester offices, but he continually inundated his editor with faxes and phone calls, as he had previously done with Mike Gabbert. Over the years Grimsditch learned which ones to take seriously and which ones to disregard: 'I've got a collection of David Sullivan faxes and I keep promising to fax them back to him because they vary so much. For example, one week he has a theory that the colour should be across the top of page one and then a week later he'll send me a note saying it should be down the left-hand side of page one simply because the sales figures were better for that day. I don't take any of them seriously unless he sends one two or three times on the same subject. Then I know he's remembered what it is.'

Despite what he calls these 'fax wars', Grimsditch gradually acquired a grudging respect for his new proprietor. 'At around half past ten in the morning he can be an absolute sweetie and by half past one he's an absolute bastard, but then so is everyone else. He's much more honest, even when he's mad, than other newspaper people I've worked for and I've worked for Mirror Group, Associated Newspapers, Express and God knows who else. In many ways it's easier to work for him because at least you know where you stand at any given time and you don't have seventeen assistant general managers down the corridor who spend their entire life backstabbing you.'

David Sullivan watched the development of Sport Newspapers with increasing pride. He told *Marketing Week*: 'A lot of experts said that what we achieved was impossible. In marketing terms it was a miracle. We have launched a mass consumer product that sells 1.4 million items a week and is worth £20 million a year at retail level without any TV advertising because the IBA would not allow us on the air. It's like playing in a football team without a forward line and still winning the match.'[1]

As the *Daily Sport* grew, it became more and more distinct from its outrageous sister, the *Sunday Sport*. The page-one pin-up and the strong use of colour gave them a superficial resemblance but, underneath the covers, it was a different story. Peter Grimsditch had become convinced that the *Daily Sport*'s novelty value was wearing off and began introducing some real news. Unfortunately, this shift in editorial policy was neither noticed nor appreciated by the paper's powerful critics. In some ways this wasn't surprising. The additional news stories were still far outweighed by the numerous nipples, the advertisements for telephone-sex lines and the continuing emphasis on sexual titillation. However, it was a start and perhaps if it had been encouraged the *Daily Sport* would have evolved into an altogether more legitimate newspaper.

It was the sexually explicit advertisements that continued to attract the most complaints. Every day the *Daily Sport* ran several pages of Private Shop adverts which graphically promoted their sex videos, sex aids and magazines. These large displays were surrounded by dozens of smaller telephone-sex-line adverts catering for everything from sex noises to descriptions of bondage and CP. There was even a raunchy classified section exclusively for escorts and massage parlours.

Peter Grimsditch didn't like the adverts but argued that the original failure of the *Sunday Sport* to attract mainstream advertising meant they had little choice in the short term but to carry them. 'If you go back to August and September of 1986, you'll find there was a whole series of presentations, slide shows, videos and gin

being poured down executives' throats, to try and convince
to put in the same type of advertising you get in any o
paper. What happened was a big fat zilch and no adverti
came. David is not a one-man philanthropic society and he's
going to run the newspapers at a loss so, if other people wo
advertise, then he will use a bit of lateral thinking and stronga
people that he knows and say, "Well, you advertise in my pap
to keep the money circulating because I'm certainly not goin
to run it at a loss." And I quite honestly don't see anything wron
with that.'

But the Press Council were not prepared to be as tolerant o
the *Daily Sport*'s excesses as its editor might have liked. Nor did
they attempt to differentiate between the *Daily Sport* and its
Sunday sister. This meant, for example, that their ruling that the
Sunday Sport was not a newspaper and should not be displayed
on newsagents' counters but on their top shelves applied equally
to the *Daily Sport*. Grimsditch raged at the unfairness of it
all:

'I don't recall any copy of either the *Daily* or *Sunday Sport*
carrying pictures of naked breasts on page one of which there have
been four or five examples in the *Sun* over the past three or four
months. I don't recall a straight lift picture from the Karma Sutra of
a naked woman sitting on top of a naked man indulging in what
appears to be sexual intercourse, as was printed in the *Daily Express*
a few days ago. I've got examples in my files of pictures from the
Daily Mirror, the *Sunday Mirror*, the *Daily Star*, the *Sun* and the *Dai*
Express that I would not put in the *Daily Sport*.'

Sir Louis Blom Cooper, chairman of the Press Council at the tim
remembers the council's concerns well:

'I think the view taken by certainly the majority and probably
members of the Press Council was that the claim being made –
this was a family newspaper – was really off beam. It was rea
daily magazine for the entertainment of its readers (althoug
those days it was only twice a week) and it certainly wasn't a f
magazine.

'What I think the Press Council said was that the nature
product was such that it really ought not to be generally a

Reed International paid for the titles of Eddy Shah's local newspapers.[3]

Portsmouth and Sunderland were initially undecided about the attitude they should take towards their aggressive new shareholder. Charles Brims, their chief executive, decided to try to be both flattering and intimidating at the same time: 'David Sullivan is saying we are a well-managed company and that we are undervalued. I have to agree on both counts.' However, he then went on to discount any possibility of a seat on the board for Sullivan, saying firmly, 'We haven't been in conversation and we don't intend to be.'[4]

Sullivan had bought the shares in Portsmouth and Sunderland through his private Conegate company and saw an immediate price rise of 12p as the market sensed a possible bid, an option that Sullivan was careful not to rule out. He said, 'I am not at all sure what my intentions are. I will certainly not launch a bid immediately. For that I would want to increase my stake to 20 per cent but that would depend entirely on the price. I regard this as a good investment. It is a very good company. They are very warm-hearted, these Geordies.'[5]

Despite the compliments, the 'Geordies' at Portsmouth and Sunderland decided, on balance, that Sullivan was bad news for the company and began looking for ways to get him out. After only a week they persuaded Associated Newspapers, one of their long-term shareholders, to approach Sullivan and offer him a substantial sum for his shares. It was an offer that was too good to refuse. Sullivan sold his shares to Associated Newspapers for approximately £2.25 million and pocketed a £500,000 profit – not bad for just eight days' work.

Peter Grimsditch, the editor of the *Daily Sport*, thought that Portsmouth and Sunderland's reaction to David Sullivan was out of all proportion to any threat he might pose. 'I think they were probably terrified of his reputation, they probably thought they'd finish up with pictures of Maria Whittaker all over pages 3, 5, 7 and 9, which is to underestimate the man.' Reasonable or not, this fear was to manifest itself again with Sullivan's next purchase, only in a much more dramatic way.

In January 1990 David Sullivan made his most ambitious takeover

THE SULTAN OF SLEAZE

move to date. Through Roldvale, Conegate and the Roldvale pension scheme he purchased a 7.4 per cent stake in the Bristol Evening Post, a large regional newspaper group. The BEP publishes the *Bristol Evening Post*, the *Western Daily Press* and a number of weekly free papers as well as owning substantial property interests and a sizeable stake in the Reuters newsagency.

Predictably, the BEP's board was completely opposed to David Sullivan's approach and quickly made it clear that he was a most unwelcome shareholder. They claimed that his reputation alone would damage their traditional family-based publications, which had always been aimed at the entire local community. Sullivan, though, was undeterred. He had become heartily sick of being treated like a social pariah and believed his business skills could only benefit the provincial newspaper group.

To underline the seriousness of his intentions he wrote a letter to Nicholas Ridley, the Secretary of State for Trade and Industry, dated 9 February 1990, saying that he had acquired a 'less than 25 per cent interest' in the BEP and wanted permission to move to 'a possible bid situation'. This was a legal requirement under the 1973 Fair Trading Act which states that any newspaper publisher whose circulation exceeds 500,000 has to get the Secretary of State's approval before taking over any additional newspapers.

Sullivan's letter had two immediate effects: it convinced all the parties involved that he was deadly serious and it forced the Department of Trade and Industry to ask the Monopolies and Mergers Commission to investigate further. On 6 March the MMC announced that they had appointed three men to examine the matter: Sir Alastair Burnet, the ITN broadcaster; Robert Kernohan, former editor of the Church of Scotland's *Life and Work* magazine; and Mark Kersen, managing director of the Wolverhampton *Express & Star*.

While they began considering the matter, the BEP decided on a pre-emptive first strike. They realized that their initial judgement, that Sullivan 'was like a tramp who turns up on the doorstep and you pay to go away', might well be wide of the mark. They instructed the *Western Daily Press*, under its editor Ian Beales, to go ahead and launch a massive campaign aimed at discrediting David Sullivan. One edition of the paper carried no less than three articles attacking Sullivan, including an editorial headed 'Beware of the aliens', which certainly pulled no punches:

> The Monopolies Commission is currently investigating the frightening prospect of Mr David Sullivan, proprietor of *Sunday Sport*, being allowed to take a stake of more than 25 per cent in Bristol Evening Post PLC, publisher of the *Western Daily Press*. *Sunday Sport* is the 'newspaper' which discovered an aeroplane on the moon, a London bus at the South Pole, assorted people with more than an average number of sex organs and a range of sleazy, soft-porn fantasies designed to titillate readers in dirty raincoats. Aliens, preferably with two heads, are a speciality.
>
> Yet, however bizarre, Mr Sullivan's interest in Bristol Evening Post PLC must be taken seriously. He has already taken a substantial shareholding. He wishes to increase his stake to more than 25 per cent and influence the running of the company. BEP has an unrivalled record of producing serious newspapers and preserving editorial independence even to the point where its sister newspapers often express opposing political opinions. Against this we set Mr Sullivan's record of two-headed monstrosities.
>
> He tells us we have nothing to fear: that the *Western Daily Press* and *Bristol Evening Post* and their weekly sister papers would remain middle-market family newspapers, untainted by his other interests. Mr Sullivan should tell that to his men in the moon. Even the mere association with him would damage the credibility of the BEP newspapers.[6]

Not surprisingly David Sullivan demanded a right of reply and was duly accorded one, though his article was completely surrounded by readers' letters attacking him. To make matters worse, his reply was headlined 'Trust me, I'm not the bogeyman that you portray' and accompanied by a picture that was almost certainly chosen to make him look totally untrustworthy. Sullivan began his response by pointing out that the editorial column that had attacked him had got its priorities all wrong by making Farzad Barzoft, the *Observer* journalist murdered by the Iraqi authorities, its second lead rather than its first and that it had insulted 1.63 million people by its reference to 'readers in dirty raincoats'. Sullivan then went on to outline his case forcefully:

> Your assertion that association with me would 'damage the credibility of the BEP newspapers' should be viewed in the context of the existing shareholders. My pension fund is not associated with the manufacture of products that medical opinion is perfectly certain kills its users – cigarettes. I do not sell them either . . .
>
> However, whilst reference is made to my request for consent to acquire more than 25 per cent, there is no reference to the fact that Associated Newspapers together with its pension funds holds almost 30 per cent of the company. This alone would ensure that I was not in any position to impose my views in any case (unless I could buy their shares or persuade them to give me a free hand). The opposition to my application appears to come from the directors and their fears are based on misconceptions. I am a substantial shareholder in the Bristol Evening Post and it is not in my interests to damage its products. I believe that those involved should be given proper incentives to increase the profitability of the company for which they work.
>
> I am not the bogeyman that you have painted me. My success has been achieved by ensuring that whatever product I market is one that appeals to the potential consumer. There are times when wholesale changes are required but the readers of the *Western Daily Press* should be reassured that on the evidence available I consider that fine tuning is required – not a new engine. The proper place for full discussion is not in this letter but readers may care to comment, for instance, on whether they would like to see a regional Sunday following the success of others elsewhere in the UK. I have always had a policy of inviting readers to comment on my newspapers. After all, they vote with their pockets.[7]

The debate didn't simply rage across the printed page. David Sullivan and Ian Beales, the editor of the *Western Daily Press*, fought themselves to a standstill on innumerable television and radio shows. One moment, though, is particularly well remembered. As the battle neared its climax, a television film report was transmitted which finished with David Sullivan saying that, in his judgement, 'the *Western Daily Press* is a particularly good newspaper'. The studio presenter turned to Ian Beales, who was live in the studio, and innocently asked, 'What's wrong with that?' A completely wrong-footed Beales replied, 'I wish I could trust his judgement', thus, just for the second, undermining his own newspaper.

In the midst of all this, the Monopolies and Mergers Commission were trying to separate the myths from the reality. They first invited David Sullivan to their offices in Carey Street and asked him to make his case. Sullivan began by explaining the reasons behind his application. He described himself as an entrepreneur with many years of publishing experience and a successful track record as a newspaper proprietor. He claimed that he was one of a new breed of strictly commercial newspaper proprietors who lacked the previous generation's more egotistical objectives. Finally, he said he was always on the look-out for new opportunities to use his skills and talents and it was within this framework that he was interested in the Bristol Evening Post.

Sullivan then outlined his view that some of Britain's regional newspaper groups had not always been run by managers with strong commercial instincts. In his opinion the Bristol Evening Post was basically sound, but would benefit from increased marketing effort to expand its core business and by selling off its peripheral retailing and property interests. Sullivan developed this idea at some length. He drew the MMC's attention to the large number of newspaper kiosks owned by the BEP and pointed out that even the company's last annual report had stated that 'this is traditionally a low-margin activity'. He then argued that, while it was possible these outlets contributed something to the newspapers, it seemed unlikely that ownership by a group without notable retailing skills was the best use of the resources involved. Sullivan ended his presentation by drawing the MMC's attention to the remainder of the BEP's property and shares portfolio, which included the new Broadmead development valued at £14 million. He claimed it was inappropriate for so much management time to be diverted away from the core newspaper business.

The MMC listened carefully and summed up Sullivan's contribution in this way: 'Mr Sullivan's overall impression was that the business and financial strategy of the BEP group reflected a failure to re-examine the inheritance of the past and develop a business strategy in the light of changing circumstances. He said he was much reinforced in his views by the low shareholding held by the directors in BEP. This lack of personal interest in the financial performance of the group might, in his view, explain the keen interest in property development and retailing.'[8]

It was undoubtedly a clever performance by David Sullivan. By focusing on the BEP's passive investment strategy and their non-core activities, he had correctly identified the company's Achilles' heel. The BEP had to admit that the performance of their kiosk business had been extremely disappointing over recent years. But, in many ways, the cleverest part of Sullivan's submission was what he had not said. He had deliberately concentrated on the BEP's financial arrangements, thereby implying that he had little or no interest in the papers themselves. He wanted to create the illusion that he was more like a finance director than a newspaper proprietor. Sullivan realized that, as long as the debate stayed in this area, he could win the argument; but if it turned into a discussion on newspaper content then he would be on much tougher ground.

The next hurdle for David Sullivan was the MMC's desire to interview Peter Grimsditch and Drew Robertson, the editors of the *Daily Sport* and *Sunday Sport* respectively. To Sullivan's relief they each said much the same thing: they had complete editorial freedom, they alone decided the content of their papers and they were trying to reduce the number of sexually explicit advertisements. These were certainly the answers the MMC wanted to hear, but the similarities were so striking that a cynic might have suspected a degree of collusion.

None the less Sullivan was pleased with the way everything had gone. He told *The Times*: 'They gave me a fair hearing. There was some quite deep and heavy questioning but they allowed me to say what I wanted. I'll be fascinated to read their report. I don't see how they can stop me.'[9] However, he was upset by the attitude of the BEP, the next ones to go before the MMC. Sullivan complained that they had made no attempt to get in touch with him whatsoever. 'It's fear of the unknown. As intelligent adults they should judge a man for himself. If they are so fearful they should come and see me, but they have never talked to me or my staff.'[10]

As Sullivan knew, the Bristol Evening Post's submissions were probably going to be the most important of all. It was up to them to justify their view that he should be legally prevented from obtaining a controlling interest in the group. The BEP's team included Michael Gay, the managing director, Ian Beales and Alan King, the two senior editors, and Richard Hawkins, a director whose grandfather had founded the company. They were accompanied by a solicitor and a Queen's Counsel. They began their submission with a comparison between Sullivan's newspapers and their own.

They described their own papers as high-quality, family publications which treated national and local news in a serious, objective and fair manner in keeping with the best traditions of English journalism. They said this was in stark contrast to Mr Sullivan's publications, which bordered on the pornographic and could not be called serious newspapers at all. The BEP team then went on to claim their readers feared that Mr Sullivan's associations with the company could lead to sensationalism and indecent material replacing accuracy in reporting and serious journalism. The BEP themselves believed that these fears were well founded and there was a real risk that Mr Sullivan would seek to change the quality of the newspapers if he acquired a controlling interest. They pointed to the events at the *Daily Star* as a case in point. Finally, the BEP attempted to refute David Sullivan's criticisms of their business acumen. They argued that the company's property investments had risen in value from £4 million to £14 million in just six years and didn't take up much management time. They also said that, while the kiosk business had been generally disappointing, it did have some advantages. For example, its home-delivery service provided a lot of additional sales for the *Bristol Evening Post*.

Helman Hunt, the MMC's deputy chairman, suggested to one of the BEP team that David Sullivan might stop at 25 per cent and so pose relatively little risk for them. The reply was brusque indeed: 'The evidence suggests that Sullivan is only ever a sleeping partner in one way.' Another BEP executive added helpfully, 'Describing

David Sullivan as a rough diamond is a bit like describing Jack the Ripper as a ladies' man.'

The Monopolies and Mergers Commission, having listened to the views held by both sides, then invited a large number of other interested parties to make submissions. Whether it was intentional or not, most of the others who contributed were implacably opposed to David Sullivan's involvement with the BEP. Three submissions in particular seriously damaged Sullivan's case.

The first was from the Advertising Standards Authority, who reported that it had received a great many complaints about the adverts carried in the *Daily Sport* and *Sunday Sport*. David Sullivan had repeatedly refused to take many of the steps necessary to improve the situation. The ASA concluded its submission by saying it would be very concerned if this situation was repeated at a Sullivan-controlled *Bristol Evening Post*.

Express Newspapers then gave evidence to the MMC about their own unhappy experiences with David Sullivan. Both Andrew Cameron, their managing director, and Brian Hitchen, the *Daily Star*'s editor, spent several hours explaining what had happened during the eight weeks of the *Sport/Star* link-up and finished with Hitchen saying that it had taken the paper two and a half years to recover.

But it was the Press Council that really put the outcome beyond doubt. It ripped the *Sunday Sport* to shreds, saying it published material which was consistently offensive and degrading and that neither the *Daily* or *Sunday Sport* could be relied on to give an accurate presentation of news. In the Press Council's view the *Bristol Evening Post*'s character would not be maintained after a change of ownership and this could only operate against the public interest.

These three independent submissions collectively amounted to a damning indictment of David Sullivan's newspapers and effectively guaranteed that Sullivan's request would be turned down. The MMC finally presented its report to the Secretary of State on 31 May 1990, saying, 'We find that the transfer to Mr Sullivan of a controlling interest in BEP may be expected to operate against the public interest. We are unable to recommend any conditions which might be attached to consent to the transfer to prevent it so operating.'[11]

The MMC advanced a number of detailed reasons as to why it had come to this conclusion but it summed up all the key points in one paragraph.

> The main public interest issue is the likely effect of the transfer on the character and content of BEP newspapers, particularly the *Evening Post* and the *Western Daily Press*. We consider that if the acquisition of shares were allowed Mr Sullivan could be expected to influence editorial policy and the character and content of these papers and that this would harm both the accurate presentation of news and the free expression of opinion. We also consider that the acquisition could harm the standing of the papers in their community and that there could be some adverse effects on circulation. The evidence from Mr Sullivan's previous involvement with the *Daily Star* suggests that his proposed acquisition could well impair the ability of BEP newspapers to hold readers and advertisers and thus undermine their profitability. Mr Sullivan's own ideas for improving BEP's efficiency and profitability were not provided in sufficient detail for us to conclude there would be offsetting benefits.[12]

David Sullivan conveniently forgot that he had told *The Times* he had had a fair hearing and immediately claimed that he had always known he would be turned down. He accused the investigating panel of being past it. 'I mean, the average age was fifty-five, sixty, and they're kind of old hypocrites, very puritanical. It's a joke that I could go to Hungary or Poland and produce a newspaper and I'd be welcomed with open arms but I want to do it in Bristol and I'm like some pariah.'[13]

Peter Grimsditch also felt that his boss had got a raw deal from the MMC: 'I was there for two or three hours which, as David exclusively forecast, was a total waste of time.' Grimsditch then observed that he wasn't alone in believing that Sullivan had effectively been stitched up. 'Even the eminent leader writers of the *Independent* and *The Times* noted that it was grossly unfair and that, as a businessman, he could probably do a far better job than was already being done.'

Despite the impressive array of forces lined up against him, David

Sullivan was still not prepared simply to back down and walk away from the fight. In June 1991 he returned to the fray, this time with two proposals. The first was that he be made a director of the BEP while the second, a more technical motion, was that the rule preventing Associated Newspapers from owning more than 30 per cent of the company be relaxed. Just before the Annual General Meeting he wrote a letter to every shareholder setting out the reasons why they should vote for him. He said, 'I do not seek to control the board of the company, to change the editorial character or content or the advertising policy. I merely wish to provide a younger, more energetic, commercial input to the company. My election will enable the company to draw upon my marketing and promotional flair which the success of my other newspapers demonstrates, and my business and financial judgements.'

Sullivan developed some of his ideas in a well-orchestrated press campaign. He told the *Guardian* that one option he wanted to explore was the massive expansion of the *Western Daily Press*. 'If I could turn it into a national mid-market tabloid selling 500,000 or 600,000 copies a day, making lots of money and creating jobs in the area, then that would be a considerable achievement.'[14]

The BEP board were sufficiently concerned by Sullivan's latest challenge to write a letter to the shareholders themselves. It concluded, 'Your directors unanimously believe that Mr Sullivan's resolutions are not in the best interests of your company and strongly urge you to vote against them. Associated Newspapers, which is represented on your board, has indicated that it will vote its shares against both resolutions.'

The AGM took place in Bristol on 8 August 1991. It was a fine day and there was an exceptionally large turnout. David Sullivan took his girlfriend, Karren Brady, along for moral support. Over the last few years Brady had become far more than a companion to Sullivan: she was now one of his most influential advisers and Sport Newspapers' marketing director. Sullivan knew that his proposals were almost certain to be defeated but still insisted on making a short speech. He began by acknowledging the weakness of his position: 'I won't waste lots of time because I am a realist and I feel basically this is a waste of time. But you have a board here whose performance has not been too good and they probably do not realize it. One of their achievements is making 109 people redundant and I don't call that an achievement. If they can run without those people, why haven't they done so before?'

As he warmed to his theme he began to weave in some of his suggestions which had been previously rejected. 'What about marketing the paper? . . . What about doing a deal with Great Western Radio advertising?' Otherwise, he warned, 'You will be back here in a year with no dividend or a reduced dividend or assets sold to keep the dividend up.' He finished with a bitter attack on both the board's attitude towards him and their limited shareholdings in the company. 'I have sat here like a naughty schoolboy with the headmaster looking down at me. Between them they do not own 0.5 per cent of the company and yet they treat us like naughty schoolboys.'

Despite his speech, only six people supported Sullivan on a show of hands, but things didn't look quite so bad when this was translated into number of shares voted – Sullivan's own stake in the company made sure of that. The final result was 1,703,503 for the motion and 10,481,380 against. Despite the outcome, this latest ploy showed Sullivan at his most ingenious. The bid for a directorship can be easily understood but the reasons behind his desire to lift the restriction binding Associated Newspapers' shareholding were much more subtle.

During the early eighties, Associated Newspapers had failed in their attempt to buy the whole of the Bristol Evening Post and had been penalized by having a 30 per cent rule placed upon them. Sullivan realized that if he could lift this rule he could sell his own stake to Associated Newspapers, which would give them a 40 per cent holding and effectively put BEP in play. It was by no means a far-fetched scenario. Associated Newspapers had previously been interested in BEP and they had already done business with Sullivan when they purchased his stake in the Portsmouth and Sunderland newspaper group. Even if Associated wouldn't vote for him as a board director, surely they would back his second resolution. Sullivan's failure to persuade them to do either effectively stopped him dead in his tracks.

David Sullivan had now failed three times in four years to move into a more respectable area of newspaper publishing: Express

Newspapers had thrown him out, Portsmouth and Sunderland had bought him out and the Bristol Evening Post had voted him out. Peter Grimsditch thought that everyone was being just a little bit short-sighted. 'I think they're probably terrified of him. I mean, can you honestly say that the managements of Britain's national newspapers over the past decades have been so wonderful? Look at the history of Express Newspapers – the Beaverbrooks practically bankrupted the outfit. You need a lord to bankrupt it but a mega-rich, multi-millionaire who came from nowhere in Cardiff, he's not acceptable. Is he not in the right lodge? Is he not in the right club? Is he not tall enough? Come on, he's a much better businessman than anybody who ever ran the *Express*, that's for sure.'

Sullivan's failure to get on to the BEP board, despite his shareholding, which now exceeded 10 per cent, and his publishing experience, finally made him realize that if he was going to become a genuine media mogul he would have to set up most of his businesses from scratch. His reputation would always prevent him from growing through acquisition.

There were, of course, exceptions to the rule. Sullivan had managed to buy the old *Titbits* title from Associated Newspapers and relaunch it as a soft-porn magazine without any problems. He had also bought and sold a stake in Capital Radio and purchased a 3 per cent stake in Transworld Communications, the company that owns Manchester's Piccadilly Radio and Cardiff's Red Rose Radio, with little or no fuss. Finally, Sport Newspapers had acquired a 50 per cent stake in WWR Publishing, the company that publishes the satirical *Scallywag* magazine, and was subsequently sued by the Prime Minister. However, all these purchases were relatively small-scale and there seems no doubt that any attempt to target more high-profile businesses would lead to a major row.

Once Sullivan had accepted this unpalatable truth he lost no time in preparing his next move. He still wanted a national mid-market tabloid, so he was obviously going to have to set one up himself. He decided to call it the *News and Echo* and, like all his other newspapers, it would begin with a rolling launch. This decision taken, Sullivan's attitude towards the MMC changed dramatically from one of anger to resignation: 'Realistically, if they blocked me on that they will block me on everything. So that's why I'm launching the *News and Echo*. Maybe if I can prove I can run a straight, legitimate newspaper things will change. Part of my motivation is to show the authorities I'm not a crank.'[15]

Peter Grimsditch watched events carefully and began to see a familiar shape emerging. The *Daily Sport* mirrored the *Daily Star*, while the *News and Echo* was intended to replicate the *Daily Express*. There was no doubt about it. Grimsditch realized that Sullivan was attempting to build his own Express group. 'When the agreement between David and Express Newspapers collapsed in 1988, he set out to do his own thing. The *Daily Sport* is an attempt to re-create his own version of the *Daily Star* and the *News and Echo* is the beginning of the path to produce a national daily and Sunday for a slightly different market.'

The *News and Echo* was launched on Sunday, 6 September 1992, initially as a weekly paper. Its editor, Tony Livesey, a former *Sunday Sport* journalist, cheekily told *World in Action*, 'It will be chalk and cheese with the other titles David's associated with. We've no 0898 numbers, no naked women, all we've got is a lively product. We've even got a kiddies' column sponsored by a little cartoon chihuahua dog. It's a totally family-orientated product and I personally wouldn't have anything to do with it if it were otherwise.'[16]

The rolling-launch technique chosen by Sullivan meant that the *News and Echo* would, at first, be available only in the Granada and Yorkshire Television areas. Livesey decided to turn this to his advantage and make the paper's enforced regionality its trade mark:

'This paper is going to be special because it is actually paying attention to the people it's bought by. The national newspapers chuck out their products patronizingly, calling them their Northern edition, yet football teams like Burnley, Bradford, Huddersfield and Halifax are lucky if they even get a mention, never mind a paragraph. We're going to be actually targeting the people that live here. We understand what these people want and we're going to give them it.'

It was a good idea but it wasn't unique and David Sullivan, to his horror, found himself beaten to the punch by the Westminster Press, Britain's fifth-largest provincial newspaper group. They launched a rival newspaper, *Yorkshire on Sunday*, just weeks before the *News and Echo* was ready to go. Its editor, Mike Glover, grandly told the *Sunday Times*, 'Regionalism is on the march right across Europe. It's manifested itself at the general election and it hasn't gone away. It's there in the emotional response of those who see the centre of power moving towards Brussels and want to regroup around old loyalties.' Slightly more pragmatically he added, 'When we've told people we will carry a gardening column based on the soil and climate of Yorkshire instead of Kent, they've all said, "Quite right. Bluddy hell." '[17]

And more bad news was to come for David Sullivan. The national newspapers, scared of losing market share, universally decided to beef up their Northern coverage. The *News and Echo* eventually launched into the middle of one of the fiercest regional newspaper wars Britain has ever seen. Livesey did his best to compete but limited resources made his job difficult. None the less, each week almost every Northern town was mentioned in at least one news story. Cyril Smith and Austin Mitchell MP were commissioned to give blunt, no-nonsense, 'Northern' advice in their columns. And, as promised, Burnley, Bradford, Huddersfield and Halifax all received their paragraph on the sports pages. But there was no doubt that the *News and Echo* lacked the verve and panache of the *Sunday Sport* and disappointed many who expected another ground-breaking newspaper from the Sullivan stable.

A second criticism made of the *News and Echo* concerned the way in which it had failed to come to terms with the rest of its family. No one expected it actively to draw attention to its sister newspapers but there was an element of hypocrisy in the way it tried to disown them. In just its second edition it said, 'Too many newspapers today rely on titillation, cheap thrills and scandalous gossip to boost their sales. We, as you know, rely on good honest journalism.' Had it forgotten who was funding its launch costs?

Despite the jibes, the *News and Echo* managed to launch and survive in the most competitive newspaper market seen in years. It might not have been the unqualified success that David Sullivan had hoped for, but it was not an unmitigated disaster either. As 1992 came to an end, Sullivan could look back with some satisfaction. He owned genuine national tabloids in the *Daily* and *Sunday Sport*, a fledgling mid-market newspaper in the *News and Echo*, 10 per cent of the Bristol Evening Post, 3 per cent of Transworld

Communications, plus a number of adult magazines and the various film rights he had acquired over the years. His dream of becoming a media mogul had moved a little bit closer to reality.

NOTES

1. *Marketing Week*, October 1991.
2. *Financial Times*, 31 January 1989.
3. Ibid.
4. Ibid.
5. *The Times*, 27 January 1989.
6. *Western Daily Press*, 16 March 1990.
7. *Western Daily Press*, 22 March 1990.
8. Monopolies and Mergers Commission Report, May 1990.
9. *The Times*, 25 April 1990.
10. Ibid.
11. Monopolies and Mergers Commission Report, May 1990.
12. Ibid.
13. *Independent on Sunday*, 27 May 1990.
14. *Guardian*, 1 June 1990.
15. *The Times*, 1 September 1992.
16. *World in Action*, 21 September 1992.
17. *Sunday Times*, 31 August 1992.

CHAPTER NINE

GETTING THE BLUES

David Sullivan has, until recently, seemed impervious to the recession that battered so many other businessmen during the early nineties. He learned a lot from the 1974 property crash when he lost £300,000, and has gone to great lengths to avoid making the same mistakes again. All of Sullivan's business ventures are now characterized by low start-up costs, few overheads and small borrowings, which have allowed him to go on expanding long after his competitors were forced into painful retrenchment.

John East has always admired the way that David Sullivan resists the temptation to indulge in the trappings of a tycoon and instead insists on running a shoe-string operation: 'He's a very clever man at controlling his businesses. You see, a lot of people have plush offices in Mayfair, beautiful secretaries, all that sort of thing. David Sullivan has always run his business with just two part-time secretaries. What he does is to delegate very well. He just pulls the strings like any great businessman. He knows how to manipulate his staff and optimize his profits.'

But not even David Sullivan could buck the deepest recession since the thirties and, early in 1993, he was finally forced to reconsider his outgoings. The most vulnerable items on the list were his racehorses and their stables at Elsenham Stud. They had not made money for several years and Sullivan had become increasingly upset about his treatment by the horse-racing fraternity, which he compared unfavourably to the welcome he received at most football clubs. Sullivan told one newspaper, 'I'm cutting down because horse-racing, my hobby for eighteen years, is very expensive and you've only got so much you can spend on frivolous hobbies. Now I've swung more into football. Football is now the biggest part of my life, not horse-racing.'[1]

Sullivan went on to say that he was angry at being treated 'like rubbish' at the country's top racecourses, despite being one of Britain's leading owners alongside people such as Robert Sangster and the Queen. He claimed that he was unable to lease a box at Ascot although he had been on the waiting list for fourteen years and had just won one of its biggest races. He even said that he was unable to book a table for lunch to entertain his guests. Ascot officials didn't actually deny the charges but pointed out that it was the same for everybody else and claimed that David Sullivan was painting an unneccesarily gloomy picture of horse-racing life.

Sullivan, though, was not to be appeased. He described the prize money in horse-racing as little more than 'a joke' and said, 'You put a pound into racing and only 10p comes back. You can go to a casino and play roulette and it would be 97p. It's always been difficult to break even in horse-racing and now it's getting impossible. I'm not going to take much more of it because owners are getting a poor show. I'd say to all of them, buy a football team, it's more fun.'[2]

Sullivan had, in fact, just spent £700,000 buying Birmingham City FC, though it's not clear how he squared this with his desire to save money. The football club had been an unlikely victim of the collapse of the Bank of Credit and Commerce International and had been placed in the hands of Leonard Curtis, a firm of receivers based in Manchester. They advertised it for sale in several national newspapers and Sullivan was one of a number who replied. Sullivan told them he didn't think it was worth the asking price, but that he would be interested if there were no other takers. Leonard Curtis didn't respond to his letter and Sullivan wrote again a month later pointing out that he was a multi-millionaire and demanding to know why they hadn't written back. Leonard Curtis explained that they would indeed contact him but only on the terms he suggested, i.e. if there were no other takers.

Despite this relatively inauspicious start, David Sullivan and the receivers did finally manage to come to an agreement. On 5 March 1993 Sullivan's master company, Roldvale, announced that it had bought an 84 per cent stake in Birmingham City. The following day Sullivan appointed Karren Brady as the club's new managing director. By now Brady had become more of a business partner than a girlfriend. He justified her surprise appointment to one journalist by saying, 'If you met her, you would be really impressed. She's got a very good business brain.'[3]

Karren Brady's appointment as managing director was a typical David Sullivan master-stroke. Brady is an attractive woman in her mid-twenties and, in the male-dominated world of football, she stands out far more than the football team she runs. As Sullivan undoubtedly calculated, the media was desperate to meet her and this put Birmingham City right back on the soccer map despite their relatively poor league position. It was a tactic that deeply impressed Terry Cooper, the Birmingham City manager: 'When Karren Brady was first appointed the press pack came running and they're still coming. She seemed to go from being a nobody to being in every newspaper in the world.' Many papers have compared Brady to the star of the Channel Four show *The Manageress*, and the forceful way she silenced one player's sexist remarks about her cleavage by saying, 'If I sell you to Crewe you won't be able to see them,' suggests it wasn't a completely unwarranted comparison.[4]

But despite Brady's obvious abilities, her good relationship with the media has recently begun to sour as a result of her heavy-handed use of lawyers when the *Observer* wrongly suggested she was a former page-three girl. A correction was clearly needed, but Brady's claim that she had been massively defamed seemed inconsistent with her previous job as sales and marketing director of Sport Newspapers, whose very *raison d'être* is topless models. The contradiction became even more striking when Brady agreed to take part in a glamorous (though not topless) photo shoot for the *Sun*.

David Sullivan came up with one other stunt that grabbed the tabloid headlines. Birmingham City suddenly announced that Diego Maradona, one of the world's greatest players, was about to join the club. He was apparently to be paid £20,000 to play in a pre-season friendly against Liverpool so that Terry Cooper could make a full assessment of his worth. Not surprisingly the local Birmingham newspapers dismissed the story as a PR exercise, with one of them adding that there was more chance of a Second World War bomber being found on the moon than of Maradona playing for the Blues.

None the less it soon became clear that David Sullivan was really very serious about his commitment to Birmingham City. Terry Cooper remembers one telephone conversation particularly well: 'During the first week David Sullivan phoned me and said, "I've put half a million in the bank. Go spend it." He knew we needed three or four new players and there were absolutely no strings attached. He was obviously very keen and wanted to make a good impression.' It was an offer that Cooper lost no time in taking up.

This type of generosity led to David Sullivan and Karren Brady both being given a standing ovation when they arrived to see Birmingham City's first game under Roldvale ownership. But Sullivan had no illusions about the scale of the task ahead. 'We start in a difficult position, bottom of the league with an antiquated ground and a horrible membership scheme that no one else is stuck with. We are playing with a few aces taken away.'5

Following the purchase, Sullivan confirmed to the *Birmingham Post* that he had been wanting to buy a football club for some time. 'I looked at Cardiff, my home town, Bradford, Watford and Leeds United. But we have gone for Birmingham because it has tremendous potential. It's a sleeping giant. I was attracted to the challenge. We saw it was for sale, looked at the books and thought if someone could get hold of it and do something with it, you could get crowds of 25,000 a week. When I looked at Bradford or Watford, they didn't have that potential.'6

As usual in football, it didn't take long for the honeymoon period to wear off. Other fans had already begun taunting the Blues' supporters by referring to the club as 'Bummingham Titty'. Then David Sullivan suddenly announced that all ticket prices were to rise substantially, though this proposal was later modified. Karren Brady explained that they had expected to raise £1 million in advance ticket sales but only £400,000 had actually been taken. She said, 'Season-ticket sales have fallen £600,000 short. And we promised every penny to manager, Terry Cooper, to buy players. He has already spent the £400,000 but we still need a centre-half.'7 Besides raising money to buy new players, Sullivan and Brady also tried to establish a generous bonus system in the hope that this would galvanize the team into action: £40,000 would be paid to each player if the team won promotion and a further £600 would be paid for every week the club stayed in the top six. The *Daily Mirror* calculated that it would cost David Sullivan a staggering £63,000 per man if Birmingham City were promoted to the Premier League.

Despite the transfers and the bonus system, Birmingham's results started to go from bad to worse. Soon they were at the bottom of the table and Terry Cooper, fed up with the constant barracking from the fans, resigned. It wasn't what Sullivan or Brady wanted but they were determined to benefit from a difficult situation. The next manager of Birmingham City would be someone special.

The man they chose was Barry Fry, the Southend manager. However, he was already under contract to the seaside club, a point made forcefully by their chairman, Vic Jobson, who told the press, 'As far as I'm concerned Birmingham's approach regarding Barry Fry breaks Football League rule 93 and I've written to them about it.'[8] Sullivan, though, was undaunted. 'Barry Fry is our number one choice and there is a job here for him. If Southend refuse to let us speak to him and he wants the job, then it depends whether he's got the guts to walk out and face the legal consequences. He'll be sued for breach of contract and we'll defend it on his behalf.'[9]

It was fighting talk and it worked. Fry, encouraged by the prospect of a £100,000 salary, took the Birmingham job. He also took his two assistants, Edwin Stein and David Howell, with him. Southend were furious and, having been deprived of their entire management team, insisted on a full Football League inquiry. Their complaint was upheld after a twelve-hour hearing and Birmingham City were fined £55,000. The Blues were also ordered to pay a further £75,000 in compensation, making it effectively the largest fine ever imposed by the Football League on an English club.

It was not an auspicious start to the season but worse was to come. Barry Fry went on a spending binge even more spectacular than the one conducted by Terry Cooper. In a matter of months he had bought thirteen new players and spent over £1.5 million in the process. David Sullivan joked, 'He doesn't need a door to his office. He'd be better off with a turnstile.'[10] But the real joke was that the results didn't change and Birmingham City remained firmly stuck at the bottom of the first division.

The team's continued poor performance, coupled with the large fine, the transfer deals and the growing wage bill, inevitably started to put pressure on the club's financial reserves. To ease the situation Sullivan transferred his shares to Sport Newspapers in exchange for their making a £1.5 million loan. He also persuaded David and Ralph Gold to go on the Birmingham board, despite their being lifelong West Ham supporters. But what was really needed was a completely new source of finance and Karren Brady thought she knew just where to find it.

Midland Independent Newspapers are the owners of a string of Black Country newspapers including the *Birmingham Evening Post* and, in early 1994, were preparing to float their company on the Stock Exchange. Suddenly, on 24 January, they received the first of an extraordinary series of letters from Brady. She began by criticizing them for constantly featuring the club but not helping it financially, and then suggested they should sponsor a new stand. 'Of the £12 million plus you make each year,' she wrote, 'you cannot see your way to investing a small percentage of this. Even 1 per cent would be a great improvement.' Brady finished by suggesting that the club might be better off boycotting the newspaper.

Midland Independent Newspapers were astonished by this outburst but Brady had barely started. On 3 February she sent another letter, this time threatening to disrupt MIN's flotation if it did not agree to her demands.

> Unless some satisfactory sponsorship agreement is concluded by Monday, February 7th, I shall be informing Morgan Grenfell (the sponsors of your flotation) and James Capel (your brokers) of our intention to write to our 28,000 computerized mailing list of local supporters to tell them of your total lack of support and financial rape of the club.
>
> I also intend to write to every financial column of the national press and to the financial papers, including the *Financial Times* and the *Investor's Chronicle*, and every broker, explaining how we believe we can knock at least ten per cent off your circulation. Clearly this can affect your projected profits and with your flotation and David's notoriety, it will receive a disproportionate amount of publicity. Barring you from the ground would not allow you to write about or photograph the team and Blues fans will have to buy alternative publications. Once a campaign starts against you the damage will be irreversible.[11]

Several days later David Sullivan joined in and upped the ante by writing, on Birmingham City notepaper, to the chairman of Morgan Grenfell informing him that a 'serious dispute' existed between the Blues and MIN.[12] Chris Oakley, MIN's chief executive, looked on in horror. He said, 'There is no question of us agreeing. We believe this is a crude attempt at blackmail by Ms Brady on behalf of David Sullivan and Birmingham City. We give them free publicity worth an estimated £1 million.'[13] He elaborated, 'Our sponsorship policy is part of our community involvement. We support charitable, community and amateur groups. We do not believe it is in our shareholders' interests to dispense largesse to commercial organizations for unquantifiable returns.'[14]

To demonstrate MIN's determination to resist these strongarm tactics, the *Saturday Sports Argus* went public with the story and published an editorial headlined 'We will not bow to these demands'. It began, 'Karren Brady's crude attempt to extract sponsorship from us invites a very different reaction – disgust. A series of threats from the managing director of Birmingham City are an insult to the club's name and a damaging miscalculation of the way to conduct business. She and David Sullivan, the club's owner, may think they will force our parent company to pay to buy their silence but they are wrong. Utterly, dangerously wrong.'[15]

Two days later an anonymous letter was faxed from Karren Brady's office at Birmingham City to a large number of financial institutions and newspaper offices in London. The letter attacked MIN but didn't significantly affect the flotation. None the less it provoked Chris Oakley into immediately launching legal proceedings against both Brady and Sullivan. The editor of the *Birmingham Evening Mail*, Ian Dowell, carefully spelled out the position. 'This is not an action against Birmingham City Football Club or its supporters. It is an action against two individuals over documents which were circulated yesterday. These were scurrilous and untrue and contained malicious falsehoods against our company.'[16]

Three months later Karren Brady and David Sullivan backed down and, while not admitting the letter had come from them, agreed its contents were 'misconceived and false in all material respects'. They also undertook not to repeat its allegations. But this humiliation was not the only one to confront them. Despite having spent several million pounds on players and incurred the wrath of the Football League, Birmingham City ended the season by being relegated to division two.

Things were little better for David Sullivan at the *Daily Sport*.

During the autumn of 1992 Sullivan and Peter Grimsditch, the *Daily Sport*'s editor, had a major disagreement over the paper's explicit telephone-sex-line advertising. Grimsditch had become convinced that the time had come to get rid of the adverts, regardless of the financial costs involved. Only then, he argued, would the *Daily Sport* stand a chance of evolving into a proper newspaper.

Grimsditch claimed that his aim was to 'change the paper so that it could stand alone as someone's daily paper'. He said, 'It is not an option not to have coverage of the Yugoslav civil war. I'm not suggesting vast analysis but you can't afford simply to leave it out because you want to be a fun paper. Since the *Daily Sport* comes out six days a week you can't rely on simply being an additional bite to an existing daily paper. You've got to set out to be someone's only daily paper.' He added heretically, 'And in that regard, we'll probably lose the pin-up on page one eventually.'

All of this was complete anathema to David Sullivan, who didn't believe the paper could afford to drop the telephone-sex-line advertising anyway, and a parting of the ways became inevitable. Grimsditch finally left the *Daily Sport* in December 1992 and immediately went to an industrial tribunal alleging wrongful dismissal.

The case attracted more than its fair share of publicity in the nine months it took to come to court. It became known as 'Wankergate' after Sullivan claimed that one reason he dismissed Grimsditch was because 'he called me a wanker'.[17] Grimsditch then revealed that he had kept 563 memos from Sullivan, including one in which Sullivan too had used the offending word. It was heady stuff and a battle royal was anticipated. But, in the event, it came to nothing. The dispute was settled on the court steps and the case dismissed.

After the settlement Grimsditch was only prepared to talk in generalities about the *Daily Sport*. However, he did say, 'I was trying to take the paper from the gutter to the kerb. David Sullivan doesn't understand the difference between running a national newspaper and running a sex empire. He is in pursuit of the unobtainable. He wants to be regarded as the proprietor of a legitimate tabloid newspaper but still insists on carrying totally unacceptable adverts from his own companies. He has been resistant for years to a change of direction.'

Despite repeated requests, neither Peter Grimsditch nor Sport

Newspapers have ever revealed the terms of the settlement, but it may be significant that, after the hearing, Grimsditch acquired a new Jaguar X JS. At the time he refused to comment on suggestions that the two were connected but, as he drove off, he smilingly told reporters, 'The thought of that fat little bastard having to part with money really cheers me up.'

Grimsditch was replaced at the *Daily Sport* by Willie Robertson, Drew Robertson's brother. Willie Robertson thought that he could increase the paper's circulation and reduce its dependence on sex-industry advertisements by giving it a more showbiz feel. This, he argued, would attract new advertisers who could then replace the existing ones. Robertson invested a great deal of time and money in pursuit of this aim but ultimately to no avail. The circulation of the *Daily Sport* fell to just 175,000 and Robertson, too, left the paper.

Andy Carson, one of the *Daily Sport*'s most experienced production men, became the paper's third editor in just six months and he claimed to know exactly what was required. The *Daily Sport* was immediately relaunched as 'The newspaper adults read' with a front-page picture of a model wearing only black stockings and a strapline declaring the paper was 'Back to its raunchy best'. The lead story featured *Colbys* star, Stephanie Beacham, and was headlined 'TV Steph's naked snaps'. It was followed up with a centre-page spread that included two full-colour pictures of Beacham's breasts. Inside, the paper claimed it was 'Red hot, raunchy and proud of it' and there seems little doubt that the number of topless women increased significantly. There was also an increase in the number of special offers from the Private Shop stables including 'hard adult videos for a fiver' and 'free' Scandinavian sex magazines.

The relaunch pushed sales back up to 190,000, but the paper was still not making money. And, to David Sullivan's horror, a decision by British Telecom further undermined the *Daily Sport*'s long-term future: in response to growing public disquiet, BT announced that from the beginning of 1994, it intended to block direct access to telephone-sex lines. Only people who applied for a special code and an account number would be able to use the service. In addition to this, ICTSIS, the watchdog that scrutinizes the premium-rate services, decided to ban the advertising of telephone-sex lines in all but 'top-shelf' publications.

Sullivan was furious. He had been slow getting into sex lines and had only recently become a fully fledged service provider through his Scan Calls subsidiary. He knew that BT's decision could seriously affect the profitability of both his newspapers and his master company, Roldvale. His anger spilled over into his *Sunday Sport* column the following week, though he was careful not to reveal his financial interest in the matter. Under the headline 'Make prude MPs' ears ring over sex lines', he called for a campaign of opposition to the new proposals.

> It looks like the number might be up for 0898 lines. Big Brother and the censors finally seem to have got their way and virtually banned adult phone services . . . It makes my blood boil when a minority of stuck-up, power-crazed politicians tell us what we can and cannot do. That's why we've got to fight censorship and tell the politicians what we think. So go to see your MP, write to him or pick up the phone.[18]

Sullivan even went so far as to claim that the new rules on telephone-sex lines could lead to the closure of Sport Newspapers. He described the new regulations as 'a great blow' and said, 'I'm genuinely shell-shocked. It's going to cost me a lot of money. But you can't change the system. I might have to shut down and make people unemployed. But I don't owe big sums of money so I'm not borrowed up. It doesn't mean I can't make the interest payments this month. It means, sadly, if something's losing money without it, I'll have to shut things down, maybe cut my paper down to a couple of days a week.'[19] He went on to admit that the recession was now really starting to hurt him. He said, 'The paper makes nothing at the moment; it's losing about a hundred grand a month, which I'm prepared to subsidize as it has made money in the past and on the hope that it'll pick up. But if that went to £400,000 a month which it would do without the phone lines, we're not in business. I'm hoping I can salvage things, but at this moment I don't know. It looks like it's going to be a pretty small salvage.'[20]

Sullivan may well have been dramatizing the situation in the hope of persuading the authorities to change their minds, but there seems little doubt that a poorly performing *Daily Sport* coupled with the end of telephone-sex-line advertising would give him a serious financial headache. However, the recent sale of his 10 per cent stake in the Bristol Evening Post means that he now has a sizeable cushion to soften the blow.

In May 1993 Sullivan finally accepted the realities of the situation in Bristol. He had failed both in his attempt to take over the group and to become a main board director. Still, the group had performed rather better since Sullivan's name had appeared on the shareholders' register and at least one newspaper thought he may well have been responsible for spurring an underperforming management into action. The *Independent* declared unambiguously that 'Mr Sullivan has been good for BEP.'[21] Sullivan sold his stake in the Bristol Evening Post through the securities house, Crédit Lyonnais Laing, who placed the 1.64 million shares with two institutions at an average price of 334p a share. It raised a total of £5.48 million. Sullivan does not yet appear to have reinvested the money.

David Sullivan is now in a finely balanced position. He has built one of the greatest English houses of recent years, assembled a cash pile of over £5 million and survived the worst of the recession. He has managed to launch a new newspaper and buy a football team. But despite all this, there is a strong undercurrent that suggests things may not be going his way. None of his papers are doing well and the loss of the telephone-sex lines will further undermine their financial position. The sex industry is not the cash generator it was and Sullivan's property empire has still not recovered its 1988 value. There have even been rumours that he has considered selling the *News and Echo*. In 1993, for the first time, David Sullivan's dream of becoming a respected media mogul has actually moved further away from his grasp.

Peter Grimsditch thinks that the biggest factor preventing Sullivan from becoming a press baron is not the recession but his own innate caution. 'One of the big differences between David and, say, somebody like Rupert Murdoch is that, first of all, Rupert started off with a damn sight more than David because he inherited two or three papers in Australia and, second, Rupert has the mentality to dictate that to gain you must spend. I think if he were ever to rival the Murdochs of this world then he would have to change his attitude and be prepared to sink in millions.'

But John Bull, the second editor of the *Sunday Sport*, is much more optimistic about Sullivan's prospects. 'I haven't the slightest doubt. I said this from the first day I met him. I'm quite convinced one day he will be a British press baron.' It's a prospect that genuinely worries David Buchan, the former *Daily Star* leader writer, who still hasn't forgotten the events of autumn 1987. 'Funny things happen on the road to Damascus but I shall take a great deal of convincing. I don't think he knows anything about papers. I don't want to get too high and mighty about the role of popular tabloid newspapers but there has to be a certain amount of serious-ness and educational value in them as well as all of the froth.' Sullivan knows that most people still share Buchan's view despite his best efforts to change their minds. To some extent, he's resigned himself to it. 'Once you're branded with a name you've got it for ever,' he says philosophically. 'Prince of porn, it's just a name. In a way I'd love to have done it in another area but you can't change history. I don't feel any guilt about it but other people do and therefore it closes doors that may have opened.'[22]

Sullivan's past does not only mean that he is prevented from taking advantage of certain opportunities; it also means that many people suspect the worst even when he does things for the best of reasons. He says:

'I can't win really. I give to charities all the time. It's like a guilt syndrome for having so much money. I also admire people who run them and work for them. The problem is, if you don't give they say, "mean bastard". If you do give, it's "he's only giving that because . . ." Talk about a catch-22 situation. I had the local kids' football team write to me and I gave them £500 and other bits since. I then got the old ladies from the local church saying I'm a thoroughly bad person because I'm sponsoring the under-fourteens who should be going to church. Idle minds create bad people, that's my little bit of theory on life, you know.'[23]

David Sullivan says that he has changed. He doesn't apologize for his past but claims that he left the sex industry a long time ago. Now he is a legitimate publisher with a string of newspapers. He has created hundreds of jobs and he pays his taxes. It's time, he says, that people started thinking of him not as the prince of porn but as one of Britain's leading entrepreneurs.

John East has no doubts at all. 'If you think of David Sullivan, as I do, with affection because I've chronicled his life over the years, then he is a remarkable and likeable little guy. There was a film many years ago about a little man who fantasized about being a big shot called *The Secret Life of Walter Mitty*. Well, if you want to sum up a little man who started in an East-End back room and became a millionaire, then I can give it to you in one line – it's almost as if Walter Mitty never had a dream.' East goes on to point out just how much Sullivan had changed from the 'aggressive little man' he first met in that dingy office in Forest Gate. 'He's calmed, he likes quite simple things. He loves his home, he rarely goes out. He has simple pleasures. He doesn't smoke, he doesn't drink, he leads quite an innocent life. He loves his mother. There's nothing really wrong with him. It's just the press that doesn't like him.'[24]

Tara Bardot, Sullivan's former girlfriend, is another of his most loyal supporters and she thinks the continual attacks are starting to take their toll. Sullivan has tried desperately to alter the public's perception of him, but so far without success. 'I think he'd like respectability more than anything else,' Bardot says. 'If he could change his life, go back to the beginning and start again, he would. I don't think he'd touch the porn business, he'd do it in another field.'

David Sullivan's problem is that he cannot start again, and he is currently prepared to alter only the image rather than the reality of his life. He squandered his best opportunity to change the conventional view of him when he allowed Sport Newspapers to develop into a sleazy vehicle for hypocrisy. The *Daily Sport* and *Sunday Sport* could have been bold and brash papers that led the fight for a liberalization of the pornography laws in Britain, arguing for genuine freedom for consenting adults in private and, if necessary, exposing those who said one thing and did another. Instead, Sullivan chose to do things like attacking Gavin Campbell from *That's Life* for appearing in *Playbirds* without mentioning that it was a David Sullivan film, and criticizing British Telecom for their new sex-line policy without revealing his own narrow self-interest. Sport Newspapers could have been the vehicle which finally allowed the public to see the best of Sullivan and what he has stood for. Instead they saw the worst.

David Sullivan is now facing some very tough decisions. He began his career by conning his customers. He has consistently used sex to advance his position. Even now his papers are financed with adverts for many of his own sleazy products. Sullivan knows that all these activities will have to stop if he really wants to achieve genuine respectability. The trouble is that all his businesses are now under considerable financial pressure and it is a particularly bad time to abandon the techniques that have served him so well in the past.

But there is an even bigger problem that he will eventually have to address. Beneath the businesses he admits to owning – the girlie magazines, the remaining adult phone lines and the tacky newspapers – lies the massive sex-shop and porn empire that he has never really abandoned. Until David Sullivan comes clean and starts telling the truth about this, he will continue to be opposed as a newspaper proprietor and remain the very rich, but ultimately unsatisfied, sultan of sleaze.

NOTES

1. *South Wales Echo*, 3 July 1993.
2. *Sunday Times*, March 1993.
3. *Observer*, 1 August 1993.
4. *Sunday Times Magazine*.
5. *Birmingham Post*, 6 March 1993.
6. Ibid.
7. *Daily Mirror*, 29 July 1993.
8. *Birmingham Post*, 7 December 1993.
9. Ibid.
10. *Birmingham Evening Mail*, 9 January 1994.
11. *Sports Argus*, 12 February 1994.
12. *Sunday Mercury*, 13 February 1994.
13. *Sunday Mirror*, 13 February 1994.
14. *Sunday Mercury*, 13 February 1994.
15. *Sports Argus*, 12 February 1994.
16. *Birmingham Evening Mail*, 16 February 1994.
17. *Observer*, 1 August 1993.

18. *Sunday Sport*, 4 July 1993.
19. *South Wales Echo*, 3 July 1993.
20. Ibid.
21. *Independent*, May 1993.
22. *South Wales Echo*, 3 July 1993.
23. Ibid.
24. *World in Action*, 21 September 1992.

THE DAVID SULLIVAN FILMS

Come Play With Me (1977)
Written and directed: George Harrison Marks.
Executive producer: David Sullivan.
Colour, 90 minutes, certificate X.
A Roldvale film; a Tigon release; a Hokushin video release.

Playbirds (1978)
Director: Willie Roe.
Executive producer: David Sullivan.
Colour, 90 minutes, certificate X.
A Roldvale film; a Tigon release; a Hokushin video release.

Confessions from the David Galaxy Affair (1979)
Based on a novel by George Evans.
Director: Willie Roe.
Executive producer: David Sullivan.
Colour, 92 minutes, certificate X.
Later renamed *Star Sex* and *Secrets of a Sexy Game*.
A Roldvale film; a Tigon release; a Hokushin video release.

Queen of the Blues (1979)
Screenplay: Joe Ireland.
Director: Willie Roe.
Executive producer: David Sullivan.
Colour, 62 minutes, certificate X.
A Roldvale film; a Tigon release; a Hokushin video release.
Opened: Eros cinema, Piccadilly Circus, London.

Mary Millington's True Blue Confessions (1980)
Written and narrated: John M. East.
Director: Nick Galtress.
Producer: John M. East.

Executive producer: David Sullivan.
Colour, 43 minutes, certificate X.
Later renamed *The Naked Truth* (*Mary Millington's True Blue Confessions*).
A Roldvale film; a Jay Jay release; a Hokushin video release.
Opened: Cinecenta, Piccadilly Circus, London, on 30 October 1980. Ran for forty-six weeks.

Mary Millington's World Striptease Extravaganza (1981)
Director: Roy Deverell.
Producer: John M. East.
Executive producer: David Sullivan.
Colour, 48 minutes, certificate X.
A Roldvale film; a Tigon release; a Hokushin video release.
Opened: Moulin cinema, Great Windmill Street, London.

Emmanuelle in Soho (1981)
Screenplay: Brian Daly and John M. East.
Director: David Hughes.
Producer: John M. East.
Executive producer: David Sullivan.
Colour, 65 minutes, certificate X.
A Roldvale film; a Tigon release; a Hokushin video release.
Opened: Eros cinema, Piccadilly and Moulin cinemas, Great Windmill Street, London.

The Hellcat Mud Wrestlers (1982)
Devised: David Sullivan and John M. East.
Directors: David Sullivan and Alan Hall.
Producer: John M. East.
Colour, 45 minutes, certificate X.
A Roldvale film; a Tigon release; a Hokushin video release.
Opened: Eros cinema, Piccadilly Circus, London.

The Female Foxy Boxers (1983)
Devised: David Sullivan and John M. East.
Directors: David Sullivan and Alan Hall.
Producer: John M. East.

Colour, 45 minutes, certificate X.
A Roldvale film; a Tigon release; a Hokushin video release.

Queen Kong, the Amazonian Woman (1984)
The Hellcat Mud Wrestlers and *The Female Foxy Boxers* cut together
  in one film.
Opened: Moulin cinema, Great Windmill Street, London.

INDEX

Sunday People, 98
Sunday Sport,
  breaches of privacy, 85–6
  circulation, 78, 83, 87–8
  complaints to Press Council,
  86–7, 104–6
    ruling, 105–6
  consultancy fees, 88
  content, 28, 76, 80–81, 83–6, 94
  Daily Star link, 90–100
  directors, 75
  editorial interference by Sullivan,
  79, 81, 85, 87, 95–6, 115
  finances, 74–5
  launch, 71–6, 78
  low overheads, 72–5
  opposition to, 76
  profitability, 72, 78, 88
  readership, 72, 79, 84
  sexually explicit advertising, 72,
  77, 84
  sports coverage, 81–2
  TV advertising banned, 75–6, 83,
  91
  United Newspapers'
  shareholding, 90–100, *see also*
  Daily Star
Sunday Times, 4, 18, 30, 85, 120
Sunday Today, 79
Sunday World (Dublin newspaper),
83

Teenage Sex (magazine), 42
telephone-sex lines, 69–70, 84–5,
130–31
Tesco, 98

That's Life (TV show), 28, 134
The Times, 112, 115
Titbits (magazine), 12, 66, 118
Today, 72–4, 78–9
Transworld Communications, 4,
118
True Blue Confessions (film), 30
Tunbridge Wells, Kent, 38
Turner, Lloyd, 93

UK Press Gazette, 79, 92
United Newspapers, 88, 90–100

Vodata Ltd., 69–70

Watford Grammar School, 10
We Made £200,000 (Sullivan/
Hardingham book), 18
Western Daily Press, 108, 116, *see also*
Bristol Evening Post PLC
Westminster Press, 119
Westminster Trading Standards
Officers, 32
Whitehouse, Mary, 16, 37
Whitehouse (magazine), 22, 25, 28,
31, 67
Whitelaw, Willie (later Lord
Whitelaw), 54
Wintour, Charles, 93
Woolworths, 98
World in Action (TV programme),
8, 13, 27, 41, 64, 65–6, 119
Wrinkle, Jimmy, 84
WWR Publishing, 118

Yorkshire on Sunday, 119–20